PROPHETIC
turning points

signature MESSAGES FROM
DR. DAVID JEREMIAH

with Dr. David Jeremiah

© 2011 Turning Point for God
P.O. Box 3838
San Diego, CA 92163
All Rights Reserved

Revised by: William Kruidenier
Unless otherwise indicated, Scripture verses quoted are from the NEW KING JAMES VERSION.

Printed in the United States of America.

CONTENTS

ABOUT
DR. DAVID JEREMIAH
AND TURNING POINT

Dr. David Jeremiah is the founder of Turning Point, a ministry committed to providing Christians with sound Bible teaching relevant to today's changing times through radio and television broadcasts, audio series, books, and rallies. Dr. Jeremiah's common-sense teaching on topics such as family, prayer, worship, angels, and biblical prophecy forms the foundation of Turning Point.

David and his wife, Donna, reside in El Cajon, California, where he serves as the senior pastor of Shadow Mountain Community Church. David and Donna have four children and ten grandchildren.

In 1982, Dr. Jeremiah brought the same solid teaching to San Diego television that he shares weekly with his congregation. Shortly thereafter, Turning Point expanded its ministry to radio. Dr. Jeremiah's inspiring messages can now be heard worldwide on radio, television, and the Internet.

Because Dr. Jeremiah desires to know his listening audience, he travels nationwide holding ministry rallies and spiritual enrichment conferences that touch the hearts and lives of many people. According to Dr. Jeremiah, "At some point in time, everyone reaches a turning point; and for every person, that moment is unique, an experience to hold onto forever. There's so much changing in today's world that sometimes it's difficult to choose the right path. Turning Point offers people an understanding of God's Word as well as the opportunity to make a difference in their lives."

Dr. Jeremiah has authored numerous books, including *Escape the Coming Night* (Revelation), *The Handwriting on the Wall* (Daniel), *Overcoming Loneliness, Grand Parenting, The Joy of Encouragement, Prayer—The Great Adventure, God in You* (Holy Spirit), *Gifts from God* (Parenting), *Jesus' Final Warning, When Your World Falls Apart, Slaying the Giants in Your Life, My Heart's Desire, Sanctuary, Searching for Heaven on Earth, The Secret of the Light, Captured by Grace, Discover Paradise, Grace Givers, Why the Nativity?, Signs of Life, The 12 Ways of Christmas, 1 Minute a Day, What in the World Is Going On?, The Coming Economic Armageddon,* and *I Never Thought I'd See the Day.*

About This Study Guide

The purpose of this Turning Point study guide is to reinforce Dr. David Jeremiah's dynamic, in-depth teaching and to aid the reader in applying biblical truth to his or her daily life. This study guide is designed to be used in conjunction with Dr. Jeremiah's *Prophetic Turning Points* audio series, but it may also be used by itself for personal or group study.

Structure of the Lessons

Each lesson is based on one of the messages in the *Prophetic Turning Points* compact disc series and focuses on specific passages in the Bible. Each lesson is composed of the following elements:

- *Outline*

The outline at the beginning of the lesson gives a clear, concise picture of the topic being studied and provides a helpful framework for readers as they listen to Dr. Jeremiah's teaching.

- *Overview*

The overview summarizes Dr. Jeremiah's teaching on the passage being studied in the lesson. Readers should refer to the Scripture passages in their own Bibles as they study the overview. Unless otherwise indicated, Scripture verses quoted are taken from the New King James Version.

- *Application*

This section contains a variety of questions designed to help readers dig deeper into the lesson and the Scriptures, and to apply the lesson to their daily lives. For Bible study groups or Sunday school classes, these questions will provide a springboard for group discussion and interaction.

- *Did You Know?*

This section presents a fascinating fact, historical note, or insight that adds a point of interest to the preceding lesson.

Using This Guide for Group Study

The lessons in this study guide are suitable for Sunday school classes, small-group studies, elective Bible studies, or home Bible study groups. Each person in the group should have his or her own study guide.

When possible, the study guide should be used with the corresponding compact disc series. You may wish to assign the study guide lesson as homework prior to the meeting of the group and then use the meeting time to listen to the CD and discuss the lesson.

For Continuing Study

For a complete listing of Dr. Jeremiah's materials for personal and group study call 1-800-947-1993, go online to www.DavidJeremiah.org, or write to: Turning Point, P.O. Box 3838, San Diego, CA 92163.

Dr. Jeremiah's *Turning Point* program is currently heard or viewed around the world on radio, television, and the Internet in English. *Momento Decisivo*, the Spanish translation of Dr. Jeremiah's messages, can be heard on radio in every Spanish speaking country in the world. The television broadcast is also broadcast by satellite throughout the Middle East with Arabic subtitles.

Contact Turning Point for radio and television program times and stations in your area. Or visit our website at www.DavidJeremiah.org.

PROPHETIC TURNING POINTS

INTRODUCTION

Thirty years ago, the world was a different place. The Toyota Camry was introduced, along with something called the Commodore 64 PC—an early personal computer. Great Britain and Argentina went to war over the Falkland Islands, and the Equal Rights Amendment to the Constitution failed to gain the required support of at least 38 states. Much has changed since 1982, but one thing has remained the same—indeed, it has become stronger and more fruitful every year: the Turning Point for God ministry.

Better known as "Turning Point," no one could have anticipated how the ministry would grow in three decades. While much has changed at Turning Point, one thing has remained staunchly the same: an unswerving commitment to the proclamation of the Word of God to the entire world. Prophecy—the blessed hope of the Second Coming of Jesus Christ—occupies the same place in Turning Point's broadcast ministry as it does in the Bible; it has been a top priority.

The passing of every day since Turning Point's founding has brought Christians another day closer to meeting their Savior face-to-face. So in 2012—Turning Point's 30th Anniversary Year—it is fitting to create a panoramic sweep of the prophetic events yet to unfold, all of which are associated with Christ's return.

There is a sad irony associated with the Church's relationship to the prophetic Scriptures. Truths that were set down in Scripture to give the Church hope, security, and knowledge of the future have been increasingly ignored in modern pulpits. And if the Church needed hope in the first century when Rome ruled the world, how much more does she need hope in today's teetering world? In fact, the Second Coming of Christ is the only certainty one can know, looking to the future. Yet, in many churches, the hope of the Second Coming is not preached—and Christians live with insecurity and fear to a corresponding degree.

Thus, this prophetic compilation study guide—*Prophetic Turning Points*—is a timely addition to Turning Point's ever-growing catalog of biblically-based resources to expand the knowledge and build up the faith of the Body of Christ. Because prophecy doesn't change, this study guide will remain a prophetic guide to the future until the beginning of the eternal state. The table of contents serves as a checklist of events yet to come.

This study guide has 12 chapters, nine of which cover remaining prophetic events in chronological order. The first two chapters are introductory: an overall "Panorama of Prophecy" and a survey of "What Jesus Said About His Return." Chapters 3 through 11 proceed step-by-step through the major unfulfilled events on the Bible's prophetic calendar: the Rapture of the Church, the relationship of believers to the Tribulation, the Antichrist, the Mark of the Beast, the Marriage Supper of the Lamb, the final and great Battle of Armageddon, the Second Coming of Christ, the thousand-year reign of Christ over all the earth, and the final judgment. Chapter 12 summarizes the Christian's responsibilities as we continue the countdown to the Second Coming of our Savior.

The event that will begin the final portion of the countdown is the Rapture of the Church. Prophetically speaking, everything is in place—Christ could appear in the clouds at any moment and gather His Church to Himself (1 Thessalonians 4:16-17), setting in motion the final 1,007 years of human drama on planet earth as we know it.

This study guide has the same purpose as the Scriptures it presents: to encourage you through the prophetic word (1 Thessalonians 4:18). If you are not ready to meet Christ when He returns for His Church, may this volume give you the assurance you need to meet Him with confidence and great joy.

A PANORAMA OF PROPHECY

Selected Scriptures

In this lesson we gain an overview of the subject of biblical prophecy.

You will find more in-depth information on this lesson in the book *Escape the Coming Night*, chapters 1 and 2.

OUTLINE

Some people believe that death is the final certainty of life. But there is one thing even more certain than death—the return of Christ. Those believers who are alive the day Christ returns will never die. Nothing in this life is more certain than the return of Jesus Christ.

I. Jesus Must Come Back
A. He Must Come Back to Take His Church to Be With Him
B. He Must Come Back to Judge the World
C. He Must Come Back to Rule the World

II. What Is Going to Happen When Jesus Comes Back?
A. The Tribulation
B. The Man of Sin (the Antichrist)
C. The Millennium

III. How Prophecy Should Impact the Christian's Life

For God, everything is "now." There is no past, present, or future with God, for He sees all things from the beginning to the end at once. As a result, the future is not an "unknown" for God as it is for us. Everything for God is in the "present tense"— including the future.

But because the Bible is a book written in human terms, much of its content has to do with that which has not yet come to pass as far as time is concerned. In fact, at least one-fifth of the Bible addresses matters of the future at the time it was written. Many of the Bible's predictions have already come to pass, such as those relating to the birth, death, and resurrection of Jesus Christ. Yet many more prophecies remain unfulfilled, especially those having to do with events surrounding the Second Coming of Christ. For instance, the return of Christ to earth is referred to 318 times in the New Testament, far more times than the number of chapters of Scripture in the New Testament. It is referred to in the Old Testament many times as well.

The Book of Revelation has to do almost exclusively with end-time events associated with the return of Christ. Two angels told the disciples of Christ that He would return to earth in the manner in which they had seen Him ascend into heaven (Acts 1:11). That simple, yet profound, statement forms the bedrock of the hope of the Church— the glorious appearing of her Savior and Lord a second time. Christ Himself is the center of all prophecy concerning His return, as the first line of Revelation indicates: "The Revelation of Jesus Christ . . ." (Revelation 1:1). "Revelation" means "unfolding" or "unveiling." The Book of Revelation, then, is the unveiling of Jesus Christ at the end of time.

JESUS MUST COME BACK

It is important in the initial state of our consideration of Revelation to ask, "Why must Christ return to earth?"

He Must Come Back to Take His Church to Be With Him

The Church is presented in 2 Corinthians, Ephesians, and Revelation as the Bride of Christ. As a bride eagerly awaits the day of her marriage to the bridegroom, so the Church eagerly awaits the appearing of her bridegroom, Christ. The first thing that happens when Christ returns is, He takes the Church to heaven to enjoy the Marriage Supper of the Lamb, the symbolic uniting of Christ and His bride to be one forever in eternity.

In addition to the revelry of the marriage supper, there will also be the Judgment Seat of Christ. After the Rapture of the Church, while the Tribulation is taking place on earth, the Church is being judged in heaven. The works we have done, and their continuing influence on the lives of others, will be the basis of that judgment. Rewards will be given for faithfulness to Christ, and loss will be suffered for lack of faithfulness. This judgment is not to determine whether we go to heaven-indeed, we are already there when it takes place. It is an evaluation of our work for Christ on earth.

First Thessalonians, chapter four, details several things which will happen when Christ returns for His Church at the Rapture. From many places in Scripture, Matthew 24, for instance, we draw insights as to the signs that will precede His coming. And I personally believe we are beginning to see many of those signs appear today. Nothing is left which must take place before Christ returns for His Bride. He could come today—He could come at any time.

He Must Come Back to Judge the World

Christ comes twice-first, in the air to gather His Bride, the Church, to Himself. Second, seven years later, He comes to earth to judge the world. He will come to take "vengeance on those who do not know God," punishing them with "everlasting destruction" (2 Thessalonians 1:8-9). He will judge both "the living and the dead at His appearing" (2 Timothy 4:1). The return of Christ as judge is strong motivation for the living to bring their lives in step with the Gospel and live for Christ.

He Must Come Back To Rule the World

Daniel 7:13-14 tells us of the ultimate rule which Christ will assume when He returns the second time. The focus in the passage is on the dominion given to Christ, rulership over all "peoples, nations, and languages." This period is called the Millennium, the thousand year reign of Christ, and it follows the Tribulation, beginning after the judgment of Christ at His Second Coming to earth. The One who

> *The Bible instructs us to always be looking for the day of Christ's return . . .with sober and Spirit-led discernment. How can we "see the Day approaching" if we aren't even looking for it? We are to investigate what the Bible has to say and ask God to help us. God intends knowledge of future events to help us "occupy" with a sense of urgency until the Lord returns.*
>
> *David Jeremiah*
> **Hearing the Master's Voice**

never ruled even His own tiny country of Israel is going to one day return to rule the entire earth. The Apostle John writes that "the kingdoms of this world have become the kingdoms of our Lord and of His Christ" (Revelation 11:15).

WHAT IS GOING TO HAPPEN WHEN JESUS COMES BACK?

Matthew 24 records questions to Jesus from His disciples about the nature of the end times, the signs leading up to His coming again. People have pondered these questions ever since. The answers He gave them point not to the Rapture of the Church but to the establishment of His kingdom on earth. Because the Rapture precedes the kingdom, those signs apply generally, but not specifically, to that event. In fact, the Rapture is like a trigger that sets in motion many events which will take place on earth immediately prior to Christ's Second Coming.

The Tribulation

When the Church leaves the earth at the Rapture, so also the Holy Spirit departs. That means there is no restraining influence of righteousness on earth. Man, without any restraining moral or spiritual influence, will create a terrible situation on earth known as the Tribulation. Revelation 11-18 deals with the events of this seven-year time period, a period of conflict, confusion, and wickedness. Believers are not destined for the Tribulation period. The Rapture of the Church is "pre-tribulation"; it happens before the Tribulation begins. The Church will be kept from the "hour of trial which shall come upon the whole world" (Revelation 3:10).

There are three primary characteristics of the tribulation period:

1. Worldwide judgment

   This is revealed in the Book of Revelation through symbols such as seals, trumpets, and vials from which judgment comes upon the whole world.

2. Persecution of Israel

   In the Old Testament the Tribulation is called "the time of Jacob's trouble" (Jeremiah 30:7). The Jewish people will suffer intense persecution during this period.

3. Salvation of multitudes

   Those who did not hear the Gospel prior to the Rapture will have the opportunity to do so during the Tribulation, and many will believe. Second Thessalonians 2:9-12 says a strong delusion will come upon those who heard but did not believe the Gospel prior to the Rapture. Those will not get a second chance. But many who have not heard the Gospel before will hear it and believe, and many will be martyred for their faith.

The Man of Sin (the Antichrist)

During the Tribulation, the "Man of Sin," the Antichrist, will be the dominant person in the world. All of the evil of Satan himself will be incarnate in this man. He is represented in Scripture as a "lawless one" (2 Thessalonians 2:9) and as a beast (Revelation 13:1-18). Both are appropriate designations for his character and his actions during the Tribulation. Just when it seems the Antichrist has caused there to be no more hope for the world, Christ will appear and end the Tribulation on earth with the Battle of Armageddon.

The Millennium

"Millennium" means "thousand years," and it derives from Revelation 20:1-6 which describes the rule and reign of Christ on earth. For a thousand years Christ will rule as king over all the earth from His capital, Jerusalem. The saints of God, who returned with Him for the Battle of Armageddon, rule with Christ during the Millennium. We rule from the New Jerusalem, which is located above the earth, and help to oversee a thousand years of peace and righteousness on earthy. Satan will be bound during that period so that peace may flourish and the knowledge of the Lord may fill the earth. Everyone entering the Millennium will be a believer, having believed in Christ during the Tribulation (the wicked will have been judged at this point). But children will be born who populate the earth during the Millennium, some of whom rebel against the righteous rule of Christ. Satan is loosed for a time at the end of the Millennium and sirs up a final rebellion on earth among those who haven't believed during the thousand years. The final judgment of the world, the Great White Throne Judgment, concludes the Millennium and ushers in eternity.

How Prophecy Should Impact the Christian's Life

Prophecy is a fascinating part of Scripture; but if we study it simply as a mental exercise, we are missing the point. A number of key Scriptures reveal the impact prophecy should have on our life:

1. 1 Corinthians 4:5. The prospect of a future judgment by Christ should keep us from passing judgment on one another now. We should spend our time in God's work, not in evaluating others.

2. 1 Corinthians 11:26. We proclaim the Lord's death "till He comes" whenever we participate in the Lord's Supper. That communion meal is a reminder that we are awaiting the

coming again of the One who died for us. The Lord's Supper is a rehearsal for the Marriage Supper of the Lamb.

3. Colossians 3:1-4. If we understand the future and the coming again of Christ, we will respond to life spiritually. We will set our affection on things above because we know that is where Christ is and from whence He will come to receive us to Himself.

4. 1 Thessalonians 3:12-13. If we are to stand blameless before Him at His return, we must relate to one another in love during His absence. Our personal relationships are affected by a proper understanding of prophecy.

> *At 17 my parents went on a trip and left me to take care of things at home. I let dishes, laundry, etc. pile up. I didn't know exactly when they were coming back, but it would be within a three-day window. At the beginning of the three days, I cleaned up everything because I wanted to be ready when my parents returned. How do we prepare for the Lord's return?*
>
> *We stay ready, so we never have to scramble around to get ready. We should live our lives as the Book of Titus tells us—in a godly, righteous way, so that we might always be ready.*
>
> *David Jeremiah*
> **Hearing the Master's Voice**

5. 2 Timothy 4:1-2. Written to pastors, these verses exhort us to preach the Word and do the ministry God has given in light of the return of Christ, at which time an account will have to be given. The return of Christ affects our ministry.

6. Hebrews 10:25. The closer we get to the day of Christ's appearing, the closer we should be drawing ourselves together with other believers. As the clouds darken in this world in the last days, every believer will need the encouragement of the church to remain strong.

7. James 5:7-8. Living in light of the Lord's return should bring patience, and therefore stability, to all we do. As a farmer learns to wait patiently for his seed to bear fruit, so we wait patiently for the final harvest of God.

8. 1 John 3:2-3. Everyone who has the hope of Christ's return will purify himself in anticipation of that event. Would you want Christ to appear at the moment you were in the midst of unholy behavior? The expectation of His return should purify our lives.

9. Jude 1:20-23. If we believe Christ is coming back, we will do everything we can to reach the lost for Christ, to pull them out of the fire. Every day that passes is one less day we have to reach an unsaved person for Christ.

10. 1 Thessalonians 4:16-18. Perhaps the greatest impact of all on our lives is freedom from the fear of death. When Christ returns for His Church, the first ones to meet Him will be "the dead in Christ." Whether we are living or dead at the moment of Christ's return makes no difference to the believer, for all who are alive or dead in Him will rise to meet Him in the air— "and thus we shall always be with the Lord. Therefore comfort one another with these words."

As we study the Revelation of Christ, may the blessed hope of His return be of great comfort to you as you wait for Him.

APPLICATION

1. Read Genesis 3:14-19.

   a. Count the number of times the word "will" or "shall" appears in this passage. What does that number tell you about the focus of the passage: past, present, or future?

   b. Prophecy is that part of the Bible that deals with the_____.

   c. What did God prophesy about the serpent (Satan)? (verse 14)

   d. What was the basis of this curse? (see Genesis 3:1-4)

   e. What did God prophesy about the relationship between the serpent and the woman (Eve)? (verse 15)

f. Explain the two "bruisings" mentioned in verse 15. What is the difference between a wound on the head and one on the heel? Who is involved?

g. What would be the future hardship of the woman? (verse 16) How might childbirth have been different without this edict?

h. What would be the future hardship of the man—and for what reason? (verses 17-19)

i. In the most general terms, what did God prophesy about the general domains of the man and woman in terms of provision and family?

j. What did God prophesy about the ultimate end of the first two humans? (verse 19b)

k. Verses 16-19 predict a "painful" life followed by death for the first humans. How does verse 15 offer a glimmer of light in that otherwise dark future?

l. How do these verses (14-19) set the stage for the Bible becoming a book of prophecy? That is, how does the entire rest of the Bible become the outworking of the prophecy in verse 15?

2. What is the ultimate connection between Genesis 3:15 and Revelation 20:10?

DID YOU KNOW?

In the seventeenth century, the term "protevangelium" ("first gospel") was coined to refer to Genesis 3:15, though the term has fallen out of use in modern times. The term was applied because Genesis 3:15 contains the first Messianic prophecy concerning the victory of the "seed" of Eve over the serpent who brought the choice to sin into the Garden of Eden. This use of protevangelium should not be confused with the second-century, apocryphal (false; not true) book called the Protevangelium of James, a fictitious account of the births of Mary and Jesus. It was never accepted into the canon of New Testament books.

WHAT JESUS SAID ABOUT HIS RETURN

Matthew 24 and 25

In this lesson we will see what Christ says about His Second Coming while speaking to His disciples on the Mount of Olives.

OUTLINE

The Olivet Discourse reveals some of the most important truths of Scripture.

I. **The Scriptures**

II. **The Observations on the Scriptures**
- A. No Man Knows the Time of Christ's Return
- B. No Angel Knows the Time of Christ's Return
- C. Not Even the Son of Man Knows the Time of Christ's Return
- D. Only the Father Knows the Time of Christ's Return

III. **The Purpose of the Scriptures**

IV. **The Beginning of the Sermon**
- A. The Near Prophecy
- B. The Three Questions

In 1843 there was a man by the name of William Miller living in New England who was an ardent believer in the second coming of Christ. Unfortunately, he began basing his speculations upon mathematical calculations. He collected all the data, analyzed it, and was absolutely sure he had made no mistakes in his computations. He announced to his followers that on March 21, 1843, Jesus Christ would return to the earth. According to reports, a timely comet fostered his delusions, so his ardent followers prepared their ascension robes, went into the mountains, and even climbed trees at midnight on the appointed day. They expected the Lord to take them home, so they climbed as high as possible so they'd have less distance to travel through the air! Needless to say, the day came and went without the Lord's return, and the Millerites went home to a late breakfast on March 22nd followed by the jeers of their neighbors.

It was a sad and bitter disappointment in the hearts of Miller's followers. He immediately went back to the Scriptures and found a mistake in his calculation. To his surprise, he discovered that he had miscounted by one year. So 365 days later, the Millerites were climbing trees and awaiting the Lord's return—and were again disappointed. Once again William Miller claimed to have miscalculated by a year, and the next year his followers ardently expected the Lord to meet them in the air. But of course the Lord didn't return according to Miller's schedule, and his followers turned their hearts away from both their teacher and their Lord.

How can we know Jesus will come again? One passage in the Bible answers that question. In Matthew 24 and 25, Jesus gave a sermon to His disciples in answer to a question—the longest answer our Lord ever offered to a question put to Him. Those chapters contain important truths, but they remain little researched and seldom preached. Wilbur Smith, one of the prominent scholars of our generation, called that great passage, delivered on the Mount of Olives on Tuesday of Holy Week, the most neglected discourse of Jesus Christ. There are three reasons why it is so important.

First, this passage offers the broadest, most comprehensive prophetic truths regarding the end of the world. First Corinthians 15 speaks of the Resurrection and offers a complete truth about it. First Thessalonians 4 gives us all the information we need about the Rapture and is the central passage regarding the Rapture of the Church. But the Olivet Discourse relates the Lord's teaching on a wide range of issues regarding the future of the world. It centers around Israel and her future, and just about every prophetic theme imaginable is either mentioned or alluded to in these two chapters.

Secondly, the discourse is not just a bunch of answers but a complete system about how the events of the end times are to take place. The material found here is not found anywhere else. It enlarges, illustrates, and confirms what is detailed in other passages; and it helps us see how the events fit together. For instance, the Great Tribulation is covered more graphically in other sections of Scripture, but in the Olivet Discourse, the Tribulation is presented in relationship to other events. We learn not only about the events but how they flow from one another. If we want to study eschatology (the study of last things), we shouldn't just read Daniel and Revelation—we need to open our Bibles to Matthew 24 and 25.

Finally, it provides the most conclusive answer for the date of Christ's return: We don't know when it will happen.

THE SCRIPTURES

In Matthew 24:36 Jesus says, "But of that day and hour no one knows, not even the angels of heaven, but My Father only." In verse 42 He goes on to say, "Watch therefore, for you do not know what hour your Lord is coming." And in verse 44, "Therefore you also be ready, for the Son of Man is coming at an hour you do not expect." In verse 50 we read, "The master of that servant will come on a day when he is not looking for him and at an hour that he is not aware of." Finally, in 25:13, Jesus says, "Watch therefore, for you know neither the day nor the hour in which the Son of Man is coming." A parallel passage, Mark 13:32, gives us one further detail: "But of that day and hour no one knows, not even the angels in heaven, nor the Son, but only the Father." The fact is, we cannot calculate the day Christ will return because God specifically chose not to reveal it to us.

THE OBSERVATIONS ON THE SCRIPTURES
No Man Knows the Time of Christ's Return

We can't set a date for Christ's return. We don't know it, the angels don't know it, not even the Son Himself knew it while He was on earth. Only God the Father knows when it will occur. All we can do is prepare ourselves for that day, for it's coming soon.

What would happen if someone could figure out the date of Jesus' Second Coming? Some people would live in sin right up to the appointed week and then clean up their lives and prepare themselves. Some would drop everything they were doing just to wait for His return. Some of William Miller's followers sold or gave away everything they owned, figuring they would have no more need for their possessions. If we knew when Christ was coming, we wouldn't be able to make future plans. Long-term relationships would be affected. The Lord did not choose to reveal to us the time of His return—in His infinite wisdom, He kept us from knowing the date and time.

No Angel Knows the Time of Christ's Return

The Bible says that nothing in either the natural world or the supernatural world knows when Jesus will return. The angels have constant access to God and are constantly awaiting His commands. Jesus even revealed that the angels will be the agents of judgment at the Second Coming and will gather believers who survive the Tribulation. Yet in spite of all this, they don't know when Christ will return.

Not Even the Son of Man Knows the Time of Christ's Return

Many people struggle with this passage. How can Jesus be omniscient and not know the time of His return? But at the time Jesus said these words, He had divested Himself of the independent use of His attributes. When Jesus said these words, He had taken the form of a man and did not know the time of the Second Coming. But when He rose from the dead and was given a glorified body, He knew. He knows now and looks forward to that day.

Only the Father Knows the Time of Christ's Return

There is only One who knew the time—our Heavenly Father. That's pretty exclusive company. I don't know anybody else who knows His timing. Those who think they know the day need to be pointed back to the Scripture.

THE PURPOSE OF THE SCRIPTURES

The very fact that we cannot know when Christ will return gives us purpose for leading holy lives. We know that Christ is coming back even though we don't know when it will be. So the admonition to us is simply "always be ready."

I remember when I was seventeen, my parents went away on a trip and left me home alone. They thought I was mature enough to take care of things while they were gone. I let the dishes pile up. I let the laundry pile up. I let everything pile up. And the frustrating thing was that I didn't know when they would be back. I knew they would be coming home sometime during a three-day period, but I didn't know exactly when. So you can guess when I cleaned up everything. It wasn't at the end of those three days, or even in the middle of those three days, I had everything spic-and-span before that three-day period arrived because I wanted to be ready when they returned. That is the whole purpose of teaching Jesus Christ's imminent return. We are to constantly live in readiness.

Jesus, in Matthew 24:32-35, told this parable: "Now learn this parable from the fig tree: When its branch has already become tender and puts forth leaves, you know that summer is near. So you also, when you see all these things, know that it is near—at the doors! Assuredly, I say to you, this generation will by no means pass away till all these things take place. Heaven and earth will pass away, but My words will by no means pass away." Jesus is telling us to examine the fig tree for signs that summer is coming. We can tell by the leaves and the blossoms that summer is on its way. The tree won't tell us an exact day, but it will offer a gentle reminder that the season is approaching. In other words, Jesus is able to determine the exact date; but as we see the gathering of signs, we'll know His return is near. That's why we study prophecy. We are closer to Christ's Second Coming than ever before.

In the fall, we see the Christmas decorations go up in the stores; and we know the holidays are coming. In Matthew 24 and 25, we see the signs of Christ's Second Advent listed for us, so we will be able to sense when His return is near. Someone has said the signs of the future cast their shadows before them. Reading the Olivet Discourse is like looking at the shadows of that day. The things we see on the horizon tell us the Lord is coming back in glory, and the Rapture of the Church will take place soon. It could be this month, this week, even this very day.

THE BEGINNING OF THE SERMON
The Near Prophecy

In the Olivet Discourse, Jesus and His disciples were walking about Jerusalem near the temple. The disciples began making remarks about the beauty of the temple, and Jesus replied, "Do you not see all these things? Assuredly, I say to you, not one stone shall be left here upon another, that shall not be thrown down" (Matthew 24:2). The temple was a massive place; it occupied a flat area on top of a mountain and was surrounded by a huge wall. It must have been inconceivable that such a grand place could be destroyed in just a few days. So they asked the Lord how that could happen. Jesus' answer is not recorded in Matthew 24, but it is in Luke 21:

> When you see Jerusalem surrounded by armies, then know that the desolation is near. Then let those who are in Judea flee to the mountains, let those who are in the midst of her depart, and let not those who are in the country enter her. For these are the days of vengeance, that all things which are written may be fulfilled. But woe to those who are pregnant and to those who are nursing babies in those days! For there will be great distress in the land and wrath upon this people. And they will fall by the edge of the sword, and be led away captive into all nations. And Jerusalem will be trampled by Gentiles until the times of the Gentiles are fulfilled (Luke 21:20- 24).

The words of that prophecy were fulfilled to the letter in A.D. 70. The Roman legions of Titus besieged and captured the city. Booty-hungry soldiers looted the temple's treasures, set fire to the furniture, and eventually carried its very stones away. Jesus' words serve as a down payment for the rest of the prophecy. The disciples had asked about the destruction of the temple and the end times. Jesus answered both questions, though the two events do not take place at once. But if He was so unerringly correct about the destruction of the temple, perhaps we need to pay close attention to His words about the end times.

The Three Questions

The Olivet Discourse is centered on answering three questions asked of Jesus. Matthew 24:3 says, "Now as He sat on the Mount of Olives, the disciples came to Him privately, saying, 'Tell us, when will these things be? And what will be the sign of Your coming, and of the end of the age?'" Jesus' answers over chapter 24 and 25 provide the most comprehensive prophetic truth in the New Testament.

1. From what you presently know about the first and second comings of Christ, fill in the following chart:

	First Coming	Second Coming
Date in history:		
Purpose of His Appearing:		
Characteristics of Christ revealed:		
Location of HIs appearing:		
Reaction of the World to His appearing:		
Post-appearance results in history:		
Your personal response to both appearances:		

2. Read 2 Peter 3:9-12.

    a. In verse 11, what is the word "therefore" there for? What condition is being referred to in the verses that precede, and the first phrase of, verse 11?

    b. What is Peter's subject in these two verses? (verse 11b)

    c. What attitude and activity does Peter say should characterize Christians prior to the Second Coming? ("_____ for and_____"; verse 12a, NKJV)

d. Verse 9 suggests God doesn't want "any" to perish. How do Jesus' words in Matthew 24:14 shed light on the connection between world evangelism and the Second Coming? What does Jesus' goal seem to be?

e. How do Jesus' words in Mark 16:15 shed light on the goal of hastening His return, and His words in Matthew 24:14?

f. What do Peter's words in Acts 3:19-20 add to the connection between preaching the Gospel, people's response, and the return of Christ? (Remember: Christ had just left—ascended to heaven—a few months prior to Peter's words, and here Peter is already talking about Him returning in verse 20.)

DID YOU KNOW?

Too often, the prayer that Jesus taught His disciples (the "Lord's Prayer"; Matthew 6:9-13) is repeated by rote as a devotional exercise. But it is, in part, perhaps the earliest suggestion from Jesus that His followers have a role to play in His Second Coming to earth. Part of the prayer is a plea for the establishment of God's kingdom on earth: "Your kingdom come. Your will be done on earth as it is in heaven." If we pray for the Kingdom to come to earth, that means the King must come to establish the Kingdom. That prayer could have been answered at Christ's first appearing; but since it wasn't, it becomes a prayer for His Second Coming. It is thus a prayer for the return of Christ to earth.

THE RAPTURE OF THE CHURCH

1 Thessalonians 4:13–18

In this lesson we learn how and why the Church will be removed from earth.

OUTLINE

Most people don't regard funerals as settings of hope—but they should be if the deceased were a Christian. Death has no permanent hold on the believer. One day every person who has died in Christ will come out of his grave to meet the Lord—and their believing loved ones—in the clouds.

I. **The Careful Preview of the Rapture**
   A. Dispelling the Believers' Ignorance
   B. Describing the Believers' Death

II. **The Certain Promise of the Rapture**

III. **The Chronological Program of the Rapture**
   A. The Return
   B. The Resurrection
   C. The Rapture
   D. The Reunion

IV. **The Comforting Purpose of the Rapture**

Prior to April, 1996, you could have announced you were going to speak on the Rapture of the Church and most Americans would have reacted quizzically—even some Christians. But authors Tim LaHaye and Jerry Jenkins have helped to remedy that situation with their *Left Behind* series of books on the end times. More than 20 million copies of the first nine volumes in the series have been published, volume one dealing specifically with the Rapture of the Church. In addition, volume one, titled *Left Behind*, has been made into a major motion picture. As a result, if you mention the Rapture of the Church, a lot more people in America know what you are talking about.

The Rapture of the Church is part one of a two-stage series of events surrounding the Second Coming of Jesus Christ to earth. Many passages in the Old Testament (like Zechariah 14:1-5) foresaw Jesus' coming with power as the Son of Man to reign and rule over all the earth. According to Revelation 1:7, that second part of His coming will be a public event, seen by everyone. It will take place in the clouds, all of His saints will be with Him, and everyone will see Him. The purpose of that coming is for Christ to establish His throne in Jerusalem and to judge those who have rejected the grace of God on earth (2 Thessalonians 1:7-8).

But Christ coming as judge is the second part of His coming. The first stage of His return is what we will study in this lesson, the Rapture of the Church. That is the moment at which Christ comes to receive His Church to Himself, to remove them from the earth before His judgment begins. The Rapture of the Church is the fulfillment of the promise Christ made to His disciples in John 14, "And if I go and prepare a place for you, I will come again and receive you to Myself; that where I am, there you may be also" (verse 3). At this point on God's prophetic timetable, the Rapture of the Church is the next major event. It could occur at any moment; and for that reason, it is often referred to as "imminent."

Two key passages in the New Testament teach about the Rapture of the Church. Besides the passage we will study in this lesson, the other is 1 Corinthians 15. But even with these two passages to work from, the Church has not agreed on the specifics concerning the Rapture. There is agreement that Christ will return to earth a second time, but disagreement on the order of events, and specifically on the timing and nature of the Rapture.

The reason the topic comes up in 1 Thessalonians is that the believers there were new in the faith and had not been instructed on such matters; they were being persecuted and were discouraged; and they were confused about the state of some who might die before Christ returned. So, in 1 Thessalonians Paul assures them that no saint, dead or alive, is going to miss the Rapture. And in 2 Thessalonians he assures them no saint will go through the Tribulation, or the time of judgment to be executed by Christ just prior to His Second Coming.

While there is disagreement on the timing of the Rapture, suffice it to say at this juncture that the purpose of the Rapture is to spare the Church from the Tribulation. The Bible says there is no condemnation for those who are in Christ Jesus (Romans 8:1), and that includes the Tribulation condemnation God will bring upon those who have rejected His offer of salvation. It is my clear understanding of Scripture that the Christians for whom Christ suffered and died will not suffer through the judgments of the Tribulation period.

Paul's teaching in 1 Thessalonians 4, focuses specifically on those who will not be alive at the time of the Rapture.

The English word "rapture" is not found in Scripture; the term is used to describe the events of 2 Thessalonians 4:17—a catching up of the saints. While "rapture" actually derives from the Latin translation of verse 17, it is ironic that the word means joy or ecstasy in English. It reminds us that the Rapture of the Church is going to be a moment of unparalleled joy and spiritual ecstasy as believers are transported from earth to the heavenlies and the presence of Christ.

THE CAREFUL PREVIEW OF THE RAPTURE (4:13-14)

The first thing Paul wants to do in dealing with the Rapture is to dispel the ignorance of the believers in Thessalonica.

Dispelling the Believers' Ignorance

Someone was once asked, "What is the largest denomination in all of the world?" And the answer was "The Ignorant Brethren." That's obviously not a verifiable answer, but Paul does say frequently in the New Testament that his purpose is to do away with ignorance (Romans 11:25; 1 Corinthians 12:1; 2 Corinthians 1:8). He said it because the believers were . . . ignorant! That's not a derogatory term, it's just a fact. They don't yet know the truth about that which was a concern to them. And he didn't want them to remain in a state of ignorance and confusion—especially concerning those who had "fallen asleep," or died. Instead of living in despair, Paul wanted them to live in hope.

Describing the Believers' Death

The "sleep" Paul is talking about comes from the Greek word *koimao*. In the New Testament, *koimao* does not mean sleep in the normal sense. Rather, it has a metaphorical meaning of death. It is used that way by John in referring to Jesus' words about Lazarus who had died (John 11:11). And it is used to describe Stephen when he died as a result of stoning by the Jews (Acts 7:60). When Paul refers to the death of King David, he says he "fell asleep" (Acts 13:36), as well as when he refers to those who witnessed the resurrected Christ but are now dead (1 Corinthians 15:6). He also, in 1 Corinthians, refers to believers who have died as having "fallen asleep" (1 Corinthians 15:18, 20).

It is understandable that, for Christians, the concept of death should be likened to sleep since the expectation was that we would be awakened (resurrected from the dead) one day when Christ returns. Our modem word "cemetery" is taken from the Greek word *koimeteria*, which was a place for burying the dead a "sleeping place." The word was also used for an inn, a place where travelers could sleep temporarily. The expectation was that you would get up and continue your journey after a brief period of rest, just as it is today with our hotels and motels. When Christians die, their souls and spirits go immediately to be with the Lord. The bodies of Christians who die are "asleep" until the coming of the Lord. At that time, their bodies will be "awakened" and united with their souls and spirits. It is important to understand that the Greek word is never used for the sleep of the soul—only the body. The believer's soul is continually awake in the presence of the Lord until the body of the believer is raised from the dead.

Paul's words are a reminder of what a wonderful hope we have —that death is not a permanent event. That is why he compares the believer with those who sorrow, those who have no such hope of life after death. The Christian has a hope which no other person in the world has. No other religion offers the great and precious promise of life after death that Christianity does. When the Christian stands beside the grave of a Christian loved one, he knows he will see that loved one again. We sorrow naturally at the death of a loved one since we will miss their company and presence. But we do not sorrow "as others who have no hope" (4:13). The tears I shed at my own parents' funerals were real—I miss their fellowship and the comfort of their presence. But I did not cry tears of despair, for I know I will see them again soon.

This passage is a great commentary on 1 Corinthians 15 where Paul says that Christ has taken the sting out of death (verses 55-56) for the Christian. The sting Christ removed is the idea that death is the end, that there is nothing more to "life" after death. He changed death to "sleep"; He made death just a temporary aside until we are resurrected and begin to enjoy the eternal life we received when we became a Christian.

So, Paul tells the Thessalonian believers, the deceased have not been excluded from the Rapture. They will be there as surely as those who are alive when Christ comes for the Church. Dispelling whatever false information the believers had been given must have brought great joy to them—as it does to us.

THE CERTAIN PROMISE OF THE RAPTURE (4:15)

Paul summarizes verses 13 and 14 with a clear promise: "We who are alive and remain until the coming of the Lord will by no means precede those who are asleep." And this is not just Paul's opinion. What he says he promises "by the word of the Lord." Here's what I think Paul means by this reference to authority. The Rapture of the Church is not mentioned in the four gospels, nor will you find reference to it in the Old Testament. It is not until we get to Paul's writing that we find the Rapture discussed. And that is because Paul got it as a direct revelation from the Lord—the revelation of a "mystery," as he calls the Rapture in 1 Corinthians 15:51.

Not only do the dead rise at the Rapture, they rise first. If we who are living don't precede them, then they precede us. The dead are first in time and in prominence, according to the use of protas ("first") in verse 16. So those believers who have lost loved ones in the Lord will see them rise first to meet Christ in the air. They take the prominent place.

We have learned from Paul so far that the Rapture is not just for the living, it is for all who are in Christ-deceased or alive. Second, we have learned that the dead in Christ will rise first, followed by those who are living at the time of the Rapture. Now, what about the timing of the events which make up this grand reunion for believers with each other and with their Lord?

THE CHRONOLOGICAL PROGRAM OF THE RAPTURE (4:16–17)

Four key events are specifically described by Paul in the order in which they will occur:

The Return (verse 16)

Verse 16 says, "For the Lord Himself will descend from heaven with a shout, with the voice of an archangel, and with the trumpet of God." When the Lord comes in judgment, He sends His angels as reaping ministers, but at the Rapture "the Lord Himself" comes. That is in keeping with what the angels told the apostles at Christ's resurrection: "This same Jesus . . . will so come in like manner . . ." (Acts 1:11). Not the angels, not the Holy Spirit, but the Lord Jesus Himself descends from heaven and catches up the Church to Himself.

There will be sounds accompanying His appearing: a shout, the voice of an archangel, and the trumpet of God. But these are not three distinct and different sounds occurring one after another. There is only one sound at the appearing of Christ, and it is described by Paul in three different ways. The passage could be read this way: "The Lord shall descend with a shout which is like such a thing as the voice of an archangel and such a thing as a trumpet of God." No one knows what it will sound like, but it will likely be like nothing ever heard on earth before. As such, it will be instantly recognizable by those who belong to the Lord.

The Resurrection (verse 16)

Paul continues, "And the dead in Christ will rise first." If you are not alive at the Rapture, when Christ returns for the Church, then you want to be raised in this resurrection to meet Him in the air. William Barclay, a commentator on the New Testament books, wrote some wonderful words about this resurrection:

"If a man has lived in Christ, and died in Christ, even if he is dead, he is still in Christ. That means that between Jesus Christ and the man who loves him, there is a relationship which nothing can break. It is a relationship which overpasses death. Because Jesus Christ lived and died and rose again, so the man in Christ shall live and die and rise again. Nothing in life or death can ever separate him from Christ."

The person who has died in Christ, and the person who is alive in Christ, will enjoy the same blessed reunion with Christ. The Resurrection is the great hope of every believer who dies before Christ returns.

The Rapture (verse 17)

Paul continues, "Then we who are alive and remain shall be caught up together with them in the clouds to meet the Lord in the air . . ." The words "caught up" are what we refer to by the word "rapture." The Greek word, *harpazo*, has several interesting meanings:

1. To carry off by force

   The word can mean to forcefully remove or carry off, and it has significant meaning for the Rapture. Satan and his minions will do whatever they can to block the uniting of Christ with His Church, but the Lord will overpower the Enemy and remove believers "by force."

2. To claim for oneself eagerly

   Another of the word's meanings implies the eagerness with which Christ will return to embrace those who are His, those He redeemed by His own shed blood.

3. To snatch away speedily

   This meaning refers to the sudden nature of the Rapture. Paul says in 1 Corinthians 15:52 that the Rapture will take place "in a moment, in the twinkling of an eye, at the last trumpet." We are going to be translated from earth to heaven in a mere moment. It will be an event that will astonish the rest of the world—millions of believing Christians will simply vanish off the face of the earth.

4. To rescue from the danger of destruction

   This may be the most important meaning of the four from the perspective of God's plan for planet earth. Believers will be removed from the earth before the judgment of the Tribulation takes place and many, many unbelievers are destroyed.

Some wonder at the unusual nature of this event—believers being suddenly removed from earth. But it has happened before. In Hebrews 11:5 we read of Enoch whom God took from earth before he died (Genesis 5:24). Then there was Elijah who went up "by a whirlwind into heaven" (2 Kings 2:11). An instance we don't often think about in this regard is Paul himself who was "caught up to the third heaven . . . caught up into Paradise" (2 Corinthians 12:2, 4). Twice Paul uses the same word, *harpazo*, to describe his own experience. Of course, Paul didn't remain in heaven, but he got there the same way we will get thereby being snatched away in a moment of time.

The Reunion (verse 17)

The reunion occurs when the dead and the living in Christ meet one another and together meet the Lord in the air: "Then we who are alive and remain shall be caught up together with them in the clouds to meet the Lord in the air. And thus we shall always be with the Lord." Let's be clear about what takes place at this reunion. The real person, the soul and spirit of a Christian, leaves the body at death and goes into the presence of the Lord. So when the dead are raised, the living person who has been in the presence of Christ is reunited with their glorified, resurrected body. That's the first part of the reunion.

Then, resurrected believers are going to meet the living believers in the air. They rise before the living do, but we all meet in the air. That means we all proceed to meet the Lord together in the air. I have thought about what a great time of fellowship and joy that reunion will be. If you're like me, you don't like to watch something beautiful or meaningful or exciting by yourself. As much as I love to watch football on television, I'd much rather watch it with my wife and kids than by myself. It's just more fun to get excited with others who are as excited as you are. That's the way the Rapture is going to be. We are going to be with those we are closest to in the Lord, enjoying the most exciting event in history!

In biblical days, when a person of importance visited the ruler of a distant city, the ruler would send a royal ambassador and his entourage out of the city to greet the visitors and escort them back into the city. That is exactly how we come into the presence of God. We will be greeted by the Lord Jesus Christ Himself and escorted into heaven. How could anyone who knows about the glory of that day not want to become a Christian and be a part of it.

THE COMFORTING PURPOSE OF THE RAPTURE (4:18)

We know the effect that a lack of knowledge must have had on the Thessalonian Christians, for in verse 18 Paul encourages them to "comfort one another with these words." They must have been genuinely in despair over the state of their deceased loved ones who had not remained alive until the coming of the Lord.

I can't count the number of times as a pastor I have stood at the graveside of a deceased believer and comforted the family with Paul's words. And what a comfort they are! It is not easy to say good-bye to a loved one, even under the best of circumstances. And if there is any comfort at all to be taken in those times, it is in the fact that we will see that person again. Remember this wonderful verse the next time you need to extend a word of grace to one who has lost a loved one. Let them know that at the Rapture of the Church, that one who has just died will come out of the ground, join the Lord to return to heaven, never to be separated from their loved ones again. If you can, read it to them from the Bible so they'll know you aren't making it up. You'd be surprised how many Christians do not know the truth about the Rapture—what will happen one day to the dead in Christ.

Paul often exhorts believers to comfort each other with the words of truth he has written. It happens again with the Thessalonians in chapter 5, verse 11, after he has instructed them regarding the Day of the Lord, another aspect of end-time truth. These verses of comfort in 1 Thessalonians are a stern rebuke to those who say prophecy has no real practical value. Whenever I hear that, I know I have met a member of "The Ignorant Brethren" denomination. The great purpose in all prophetic texts is to give hope to the believer, to let the believer know that God has a plan and a purpose in the future. When you are suffering, either for the sake of the Gospel as the Thessalonians were, or for any reason, it is a great comfort to know that heaven awaits you. And if you've been separated from loved ones by death, the same reality applies. This life is not all there is! We look for the day when we will be united with the rest of the Church and our Lord Jesus Christ. If that is not a comfort, what could be?

Two applications flow naturally from this great passage of Scripture. First, be looking for the Lord. As already stated, the Rapture of the Church is the next event on God's prophetic agenda. It could happen before you finish reading this lesson. Are you ready? Second, be living for the Lord. Just because we know the Lord could return at any moment is no reason to fold our hands and wait. I want to be found abounding in the work of the Lord when He returns (1 Corinthians 15:58), not relaxing in the midst of a perishing world.

Please join me today in looking and living for the Lord who is soon to appear in the clouds. What a day that will be!

APPLICATION

1. Read Zechariah 14:1–7.

   a. What is the topic of this passage? (verse 1a)

   b. What will the nations do in that "day"? (verse 2)

   c. What will the Lord do to defend Jerusalem? (verse 3)

   d. What dramatic event will take place in Jerusalem? (verse 4)

   e. What role will the saints of God play? (verse 5)

f. Note as many differences/similarities as you can between this event and the event Paul describes in 1 Thessalonians 4:13–18 (location, key figures, the role of the saints, etc.).

2. Read John 14:1–4.

   a. What parallel do you find in verse 1 with 1 Thessalonians 4:18?

   b. How might Christ's role as the One who goes ahead of you give you encouragement in dealing with unknown issues in your life?

   c. At this moment, what does Christ have prepared for you in heaven? (verse 3)

   d. What do you think could prevent you from occupying that place one day?

The next time you are in a cemetery, especially an older one, see how many of the graves are oriented in an East-West direction—with the foot of the grave pointing to the east. It was customary in cemeteries, especially those associated with a church, for the graves to face the east. This was because of the ancient tradition that said when the Lord returns to establish His kingdom, He will enter through the Eastern Gate across the Kidron Valley from the Mount of Olives in Jerusalem. This was the gate through which Ezekiel saw the glory of the Lord depart (Ezekiel 10:18–19) and prophetically return (Ezekiel 43:4, and through which Jesus likely entered Jerusalem at His "triumphal entry."

THE BELIEVER AND THE TRIBULATION

1 Thessalonians 5:1–11

In this lesson we learn about the coming Day of the Lord.

OUTLINE

Most people don't like surprises; they prefer the peace and security of an uninterrupted way of life. But the world is headed toward a "surprise" of global proportions, a day in which true peace and security will be found by Christians, and upheaval by those who do not believe.

I. **The Secrecy of the Times**

II. **The Suddenness of His Return**
   A. The False Security
   B. The Sudden Destruction
   C. The Failure to Escape

III. **The Safety of the Believers**
   A. The Difference Christians Embody
   B. The Darkness Christians Escape
   C. The Distinction Christians Express

IV. **The Seriousness of Believers**
   A. A Call to Be Alert
   B. A Call to Be Armed

V. **The Salvation of Believers**
   A. The Doctrine That Encourages Us
   B. The Duty That Empowers Us

The Rapture of the Church results in two things: It brings to a conclusion the age of grace whereby believers have been able to freely receive Christ by grace through faith (Ephesians 2:8–9). It also signals the beginning of the most horrendous period of time planet earth has ever experienced, the Tribulation. This is a seven-year period when the Holy Spirit is absent from earth and great judgments are unleashed. The last three-and-a-half years are known as the Great Tribulation when the plagues and destruction are intensified and climaxed by the Battle of Armageddon. The Church is absent form this terrible period of time as a result of the Rapture.

The Rapture and the Tribulation begin a period of time which the Old Testament prophets referred to a s the Day of the Lord. Given the detailed revelation conveyed to New Testament writers, we now know more than the prophets of old did. The Day of the Lord extends from the Rapture, through the Tribulation, through the Millennium and concludes with the Great White Throne Judgments —after which God's eternal kingdom begins. The Day of the Lord, therefore, encompasses all the end-time events yet remaining on God's prophetic calendar.

The perspective of the Old Testament prophets was focused primarily on the Tribulation, the time of trouble coming upon the earth ("the time of Jacob's trouble"; Jeremiah 30:7). Numerous Scriptures in the Old Testament refer to the Day of the Lord, and do so in a context of judgment and trouble: Isaiah 2:12; 13:9; 61:2; Jeremiah 30:7; Joel 2:1–2a; Amos 5:18–20; Zephaniah 1:14–18; Malachi 4:1. And those are just representative; there are many more which speak of the bleak times that are coming upon the earth in the days ahead. Every person you know who is not a born-again Christian will be on earth during that time to experience the judgments and troubles which are coming. Only Christians will be spared the agony.

Having set the stage, we come to Paul's words beginning in 1 Thessalonians, chapter five. Here he continues on the theme of chapter four, the Rapture, by giving information and exhortation on the Day of the Church, which is why Paul begins his reference to it in chapter five.

THE SECRECY OF THE TIMES (5:1–2)

The Believers in Thessalonica were concerned about the fate of their deceased loved ones±believers who had already died and would therefore miss the return of Christ. Paul explained in 4:13–18 that believers who died prior to Christ's return would be raised to meet

Him at the Rapture. Now, the believers apparently have another question: When will the Day of the Lord take place?

When Paul says, "you have no need that I should write to you" (verse 1), it is because they already know (generally) "the times and the seasons." He had just explained it to them in chapter four. When the Rapture takes place, the Day of the Lord begins.

The "times and seasons" is a phrase used three times in the Bible to refer to God's plans for Israel and the nations (Daniel 2:21; Acts 1:7; 1 Thessalonians 5:1). He has not revealed to us the exact schedule for those events which remain, but there is a schedule. Acts 17:26 says God "has determined [the nations'] preappointed times and the bounderies of their dwellings." But Paul tells the Thessalonians they don't need to know the exact times and seasons. What we do need to know is that the events are coming in order that we might be prepared for them. We need only be concerned with what we can control—and that is our choices and responses regarding the events we know are coming.

Though Paul doesn't lay all this out in as much detail, it will help in our study to pull together what we glean from all of Scripture about the events of the Day of the Lord. First comes the Rapture of the Church (living and dead saints meeting Christ in the air), then the seven-year Tribulation (the second half of which is the Great Tribulation; the Church is in heaven during this period), then the Second Coming of Christ physically to the earth. Revelation 19:11–16 details in specific terms what the Second Coming will be like. Then, verses 17–21 spell out the judgment God will send upon the nations who have opposed Him and have made war against Israel during the Tribulation. The armies of the nations of the earth will be destroyed, and the birds of heaven will come and eat the flesh of the dead. It is a gruesome end to the most horrific period of earth's history.

Sometimes people ask me why God allows all the idolatry and immorality and heathenism and atheism to take place unabated on earth. It seems as if God is unaware of what is happening. No, He is not unaware. Rather, He has planned for His judgment to take place at a certain time, a day in which all accounts will be settled. Christ Himself referred to God's coming judgments, associated with the Day of the Lord, in Matthew 24:21–22.

There are some differing views in the Body of Christ about when the Rapture of the Church takes place relative to the Tribulation and Second Coming. Some, called Post-Tribulationists, believe the Rapture occurs simultaneously with the Second Coming at the end of the Tribulation. In other words, the Church goes through the Tribulation along with everyone else, then is translated into the air to meet the Lord as He returns at the Second Coming. Others say the Rapture occurs at the mid-point of the Tribulation; they are called Mid-Tribulationists.

I believe the Bible teaches that Christians will be saved from the wrath which is coming upon the earth (Revelation 3:10). Since Christ died on the cross for us, "There is therefore now no condemnation to those who are in Christ Jesus" (Romans 8:1). Why would Christ die to save us from judgment if we were then expected to endure judgment in the Tribulation? The wrath and judgment of the Tribulation is upon nonbelievers, not believers. There is no reason for the Church to be on the earth during that period. This is the Pre-Tribulation view.

The final word Paul gives about the Day of the Lord is that it will begin "as a thief in the night" (5:2). Paul's point is that we do not, and will not, know when the Rapture will occur (the beginning of the Day of the Lord). Thieves don't give advance notice of their appearance. They come unexpectedly which is how the Rapture will occur. The metaphor of a thief in the night is used frequently in Scripture to illustrate "unexpectedness" in the Day of the Lord (Matthew 24:42–43; 2 Peter 3:10; Revelation 3:3; 16:15).

The return of Christ at the Rapture, and the initiation of the Day of the Lord, will be a secret event. Anyone who says he has figured out when the return of Christ will be is wrong. No one knows! When Jesus was on earth He said neither the angels nor He knew (Matthew 24:36). Only the Father (and now Jesus, since He is with the Father in heaven) knows the day and the time of the Son's return.

THE SUDDENNESS OF HIS RETURN (5:3)

Not only is the return of Christ at the Rapture going to be secret, it is going to be sudden. The world is going to be living in a state of false security, a state of supposed "peace and safety" (5:3). Just as a woman is in peace one minute and in the anguished throes of labor pains the next, so the world will suddenly be jolted by the return of Christ.

The False Security

We generally think of the end times as being a period of declining peace, increased evidence of godlessness on the earth. But there will apparently be a sense in which people are led to believe everything is okay—a day of "peace and safety." This is the way it was just before the flood in Noah's day. People were going about their lives as if judgment were far from them (Matthew 24:38). There was a 120-year period during which preaching was taking place but no one was listening except Noah and his family (Genesis 6:3; 1 Peter 3:20). It was the same in Lot's day when he lived in Sodom and Gomorrah. The Lord sent men to warn Lot of the impending judgment, but some in Lot's family thought he was joking (Genesis 19:12–14). They didn't believe him; they thought everything was fine.

When I hear preachers say that teaching and preaching about prophecy isn't relevant to where Christians live, I think to myself, "Five minutes after the Rapture it's going to be very relevant." Since the Rapture could occur at any moment, nothing could be more relevant. The only warning that will be given about the return of Christ is the warning you are reading right now—the teaching and preaching of what the Word of God says about prophecy and future events. Otherwise, the Rapture is going to be a secret and sudden event.

The Sudden Destruction

Without going into lots of graphic detail about labor pains, let me make Paul's point succinctly: The return of Christ is inevitable! That is, every woman knows that when labor pains begin, the birth process has started and the soon appearance of a child is inevitable. Even though the birth pangs are happening, the mother doesn't know the exact moment the baby will appear. Suddenly, the baby is born! The pain of childbirth is severe and the timing is sudden, both of which characterize the coming of the Lord at the Rapture. And no one will escape the destruction which follows in the Day of the Lord.

The Failure to Escape

In Daniel 5 we read about the feast held by Belshazzar in Babylon, using the utensils and vessels which had been taken from the temple in Jerusalem. He desecrated those sacred items of worship in his pagan revelry, mocking the God of Israel as if to say, "We are in control. God has not stopped us from what we are doing!" That very night, Belshazzar, king of the Chaldeans, was killed (Daniel 5:30). Just when he thought he had everything under control, God stepped in and demonstrated who is really in control.

It's the same thing in Acts 12. Herod put Peter in jail for preaching, and God promptly delivered him—and then put Herod to death by sending an angel of the Lord to destroy him (Acts 12:23). The people were praising Herod as if he were a god and "immediately" God stepped in to show who is really God. And then there was the rich man in one of Jesus' parables who boasted of all his wealth—and then lost it as God required his soul of him that every night (Luke 12:20).

God's pattern is to bring destruction suddenly, and it is an inescapable destruction. People will be going through their day, a day just like today, watching television and driving car pools and doing their jobs—and suddenly millions of people all over the world will vanish. The Rapture will occur and then the destruction of the Tribulation will begin. It will all happen suddenly, and there will be no escape.

THE SAFETY OF THE BELIEVERS (5:4)

Thankfully, believers will be removed to safety before the judgment on earth begins. Notice that verse four begins with "But" —meaning there is a contrast with what has preceded it. The end of verse three says, "They shall not escape" the sudden destruction. But . . . the contrast is to the believers who are not living in darkness and who will not be overtaken by the destruction which will come as a thief in the night. That day will not catch believers by surprise because we will be in heaven with Christ who has rescued us from that coming judgment at the Rapture.

The Difference Christians Embody

Paul sets up a distinguishing difference between the future of believers and unbelievers in these verses by his use of contrasting pronouns: "you" and "they." There are only two categories of people on earth. Those upon whom the day of destruction will come and those upon whom it will not come. The difference between "us" and "them" is a relationship with Christ which removes us from the coming judgment.

The Darkness Christians Escape

"But you, brethren, are not in darkness" (5:4). The reason Christians escape darkness is because "God did not appoint us to wrath, but to obtain salvation through our Lord Jesus Christ" (5:9). We are reminded once again that God has something far better in store for His children than to suffer the wrath for sin from which the cross of Christ has already delivered them.

The Distinction Christians Express

What sets Christians apart is that we are of the day (light), not of the night (darkness). In fact, Colossians 1:13 says we have been rescued from darkness and brought into the light. Darkness speaks of those who have not believed in Christ, who still live in spiritual blindness, not having seen the light of the Gospel. Because we are not children of darkness, our lives should be different (Romans 13:12–14). We know what the life of darkness is like since we were saved out of that life. But now we are to walk as children of light (Ephesians 5:8).

THE SERIOUSNESS OF BELIEVERS (5:6–8)

Christians have a serious responsibility while we live in this world, waiting on the appearing of Jesus Christ. We are not just to be happy-go-lucky; we are to be about accomplishing that which is ours to do.

A Call to Be Alert (5:6–7)

The call to alertness in verses six and seven refers to moral alertness (not physical alertness, watching for the appearing of Christ in the heavens). We are to be sober and serious about our calling as Christians. It's possible to be spiritually drunk on this world in addition to being physically drunk on alcohol—sports, entertainment, materialism, prestige, power, popularity. Those are just as intoxicating as alcohol. But Christians are to be sober and alert. Paul is not a killjoy, but he is serious about his calling and the times in which we live. Even in the midst of difficulties, he does not lose sight of his purpose. Outlook on the present and future is what determines his steps. The unsaved of this world are not like that. The judgment of God hangs over them. They should be living soberly and seriously, but they are not.

A Call to Be Armed (5:8)

Here Paul echoes the list of spiritual armor found in Ephesians 6, but in a more concise fashion. The breastplate protects the heart, the seat of affections, whereas the helmet protects the mind and its thoughts. Therefore, both the heart and the mind need to be protected while living in a dark world, waiting on the appearing of Jesus Christ.

THE SALVATION OF BELIEVERS (5:9–11)

The final section of chapter five is about our duty and our doctrine in the final days before the Day of the Lord.

The Doctrine That Encourages Us (5:9–10)

There are two ways in which doctrine is vitally important in maintaining our vigilance and spiritual sobriety in the last days.

1. We are to be encouraged by His purpose for us (5:9).

   The doctrine of the Word of God says we have not been appointed to wrath but to obtain salvation through faith in Christ. In light of the abundant words in Scripture on the darkness of the last days, and the terrible judgments coming upon the earth, this should be a highly encouraging truth to take hold of. It is not God's purpose for believers to go through the judgment of the Tribulation. It is His purpose for us to be saved from judgment upon sin.

2. We are to be encouraged by His provision for us (5:10).

Here Paul makes reference back to the earlier question of the Thessalonians about deceased believers. God has made provision for us, whether we are dead or alive at the time of Christ's return, to live together with Christ by whom we have been saved. Once a person is in Christ, he is in Christ forever. Dying does not take one out of Christ. Salvation is an eternal, unchanging provision of God whereby we are saved from Tribulation by the Rapture whether we are dead or living. Beginning with the Rapture, we are in Christ and with Christ in heaven, and with Him when He returns at the Second Coming.

The Duty That Empowers Us (5:11)

If you want to know what you are supposed to do with these doctrines, these truths about the Day of the Lord, it is in verse 11: "Comfort each other and edify one another."

1. Empowered to break down fears.

Living in the days of Roman persecution, the Thessalonian believers probably wondered if they might be in the Day of the Lord, given the persecution they were enduring. But they were not. Paul was comforting them by telling the truth about their destiny as believers. They were not going to go through the Day of the Lord on earth. He said the same thing at the end of chapter four: "Therefore comfort one another with these words" (4:18). The Rapture has not bypassed those believers who have died, and the Day of the Lord has not yet come. It is our duty to comfort one another with these words. And especially to reach out to those who have no comfort, who are still living in darkness, whom the Rapture will pass by and the Day of the Lord will consume.

2. Empowered to build up our faith.

The next time you are with someone who has lost a believing loved one, or who is going through a difficult time, strengthen their faith through these words Paul has written here. You can tell them their loved one will come out of the ground at the Rapture of the Church and be reunited with the Lord, and with his family. You can tell a suffering person that God has not appointed believers to suffer condemnation or judgment and that they will be removed from this earth before the real judgment begins. God has a purpose for believers which needs to be kept before them when faith grows weak. Therefore we should build up one another's faith.

We cannot conclude this lesson without coming to grips with the fact that God has planned a judgment time for all those on planet earth who reject Him. And that means we ought to be busy trying, in every way possible, to introduce people to Jesus Christ so they might repent of their sins and be spared the coming judgment of God. I ask you, dear reader, the same as I ask myself and the members of my church. How long has it been since you approached someone who does not know Christ and shared the Gospel with him? Or, if you don't feel adequately equipped to do that, how long has it been since you invited them to church where they could hear the Gospel preached?

Believe me—these questions have nothing to do with getting people onto church rolls in order to grow the church. My burden is the coming Day of the Lord when all who do not know Christ will be left behind at the Rapture to endure the coming Great Tribulation. How are they going to be spared that coming judgment if someone does not tell them about Jesus? If we do not put an arm of love around their shoulder and invite them to the kingdom of God, who will? I cannot, nor can any pastor, present the Gospel on Sunday to people who are not in attendance. I love to teach the believers in my church the Word of God, but I also know there is a dire need to present the Gospel to unbelievers—those who are destined to experience the coming Day of the Lord.

It could be your effort this coming Sunday that results in a person hearing the Gospel and coming to gain faith and assurance that his life is secure in Christ that whatever judgments are destined to come upon this world—they will not touch him. We must step back at times and recognize that we have become far too comfortable with our place in the pew. There are many millions outside the church walls who have not experienced Christ and who may not unless we reach out to them and invite them to Him. If you know you will be joining Christ at the Rapture and in heaven during the Day of the Lord, pray that God will lead you to at least one other person who needs that same comfort and assurance.

APPLICATION

1. Read Isaiah 2:6–22.

   a. What is the position God took in Isaiah's day toward His chosen people? (verse 6a)

   b. What caused God to take a position of judgment toward Israel? (verses 6b–9)

   c. What will the disobedient do one day? (verse 10)

   d. What does Isaiah call the "day" when God comes forth in the earth? (verse 12)

   e. What is the purpose of that day? (verses 11–12)

   f. Interpret this apocalyptic Old Testament language in modern terms, describing in your own words what the purpose of the "Day of the Lord" is.

2. Read Hebrews 12:25–29.

   a. What warning is the writer issuing? (verse 25a)

   b. Who "spoke on earth"? (See Hebrews 12:18–21; Exodus 19:18.)

   c. What is the point of referencing the terror of God at Mt. Sinai? (verse 25b)

   d. What ahs God promise yet to do (verse 26)

   e. What does the Hebrews author say is going to happen at the final shaking of the earth? (verse 27)

   f. What should be our response to being the recipients of the kingdom? (Hebrews 12:28)

   g. Why should we have "reverence" and "fear" toward God? (verse 29)

Though when Jesus was on earth He did not know the day or the hour of the Day of the Lord (Matthew 24:36), He did give one clue: "This gospel of the kingdom will be preached in all the world as a witness to all the nations, and then the end will come" (Matthew 24:14). In some way, the fulfilling of the Great Commission (Matthew 28:18–20) is linked to the end of the age. This link provides added motivation for the Church to spread the Gospel—not only for the salvation of those who haven't believed, but to hasten the day of the appearing of Christ for the Church.

WHEN ONE MAN RULES THE WORLD

Selected Scriptures

In this lesson we meet the man who will unleash hell on earth.

OUTLINE

History is full of the names of infamous tyrants who brutalized people for their own gain. Modern memory is scarred by the likes of Hitler. But a man is coming in the future who will make the brutes of the past seem tame. He is the opposite of Jesus Christ: the Antichrist.

I. **The Personality of the Coming World Ruler**
   A. He Will Be a Charismatic Leader
   B. He Will Be a Cunning Leader
   C. He Will Be a Cultic Leader
   D. He Will Be a Cruel Leader

II. **The Profile of the Coming World Ruler**
   A. His Inconspicuous Profile

III. **The Program of the Coming World Ruler**

When I first began to preach the Bible in full-time ministry, I never shied away from the prophetic portions. I gave them equal time and emphasis as part of the "whole counsel of God" (Acts 20:27). But I do have a secret confession to make: Forty years ago I could not imagine how one individual could rise to such a place of prominence and power as the Bible ascribes to the coming Antichrist. We didn't think of the world as a "global village" at that time in history. But today the world is "shrinking"—we are connected by money, media, missiles, and materials as never before. Today, the idea of a one-world ruler seems totally plausible and becomes more so every day.

The crisis events of the end-times—not the least of which will be the instantaneous disappearance of hundreds of millions of Christians from around the world at the Rapture of the Church—will create an environment ripe for a charismatic individual to step forward and lead the world to a place of momentary stability. That man will be the Antichrist—Satan's superman. Instead of saving the world, he will lead it to the final battle of history, the Battle of Armageddon, where he and his forces will be defeated by the returning King of Kings, Jesus Christ. But prior to that time, he will demonstrate super-human (supernatural) powers such as the world has never seen (except in Jesus).

The Antichrist is mentioned in Scripture by way of several aliases: "the prince that shall come" (Daniel 9:26 KJV), "a king of fierce countenance" (Daniel 8:23 KJV), "a master of intrigue" (Daniel 8:23 NIV), "a despicable man" (Daniel 11:21 NLT), "this worthless shepherd" (Zechariah 11:16-17 NLT), "the man of destruction" (2 Thessalonians 2:3 GOD'S WORD), "the man of lawlessness" (2 Thessalonians 2:3 NIV), "this evil man" (2 Thessalonians 2:9 NLT), "the beast" (Revelation 13:2 NIV), and, of course, "the Antichrist" (1 John 2:18; 4:3).

Based on the number "666" in Revelation 13:18, many attempts have been made in history to identify who the Antichrist is or will be. Using a system of numerology where letters of the alphabet are assigned numerical values, attempts have been made to find the names of historical figures the letters of whose names add up to 666. Surprisingly, many names have qualified mathematically. The only problem is that none have turned out to be the Antichrist.

The Bible does not tell us who the Antichrist will be. In fact, Paul writes in 2 Thessalonians 2 that this coming world leader will not be revealed until after the Rapture of the Church (verse 3). So if you are here when the Antichrist is revealed, you will have been left behind by the Rapture.

THE PERSONALITY OF THE COMING WORLD RULER

We may not know who this world leader will be, but we do know what he will be: charismatic, cunning, cultish, and cruel.

He Will Be a Charismatic Leader

Three times in Daniel 7 we are told that this man will speak "pompous words" ("boastful words" in some other translations; verses 8, 20, 25). In Revelation 13:5 we are told that "he was given a mouth speaking great things and blasphemies." He will be one of the most powerful orators the world has ever known and will use that skill to sway masses of people in the direction he wants them to go. Here is a description written by Charles Colson of a similar power possessed by Nazi dictator Adolf Hitler:

> Solemn, symphonic music began the set up. The music then stopped. A hush prevailed and a patriotic anthem began. And from the back, walking slowly down the wide central aisle strutted Hitler. Finally the führer himself rises to speak, beginning in a low velvet voice which makes the audience unconsciously lean forward to hear. He begins to speak of his love for Germany and gradually his pitch increases and increases until he reaches a screaming crescendo, but his audience does not mind because they are all standing on their feet and screaming with him.[1]

Anyone who has ever seen documentary film footage of Hitler speaking in those pre-World War II rallies in Germany knows the scene—and has experienced the chills of fear in watching a human being exercise that kind of power over people. Whereas Hitler had the power to captivate a nation, the Antichrist will have power to captivate the whole world.

He Will Be a Cunning Leader

Daniel 7:8 reveals another aspect of his ability: "I was considering the horns, and there was another horn, a little one, coming up among them, before whom three of the first horns were plucked out by the roots." Substitute "kings" for "horns" and you'll have an idea of the Antichrist's power to elevate himself by destroying others. He deposes three kings as he claws his way to power in that part of the world until he ultimately controls the whole Western world. Here's another view of his ability: "But he shall come in peaceably, and seize the kingdom by intrigue" (Daniel 11:21). Intrigue and cunning—the traits of a person who is the opposite of the true Christ.

He Will Be a Cultic Leader

He will demonstrate a religious-like fervor to attract followers to himself and away from God: "He shall speak pompous words against the Most High, shall persecute the saints of the Most High, and shall intend to change times and law." He will "[oppose] and [exalt] himself above all that is called God or that is worshipped, so that he sits as God in the temple of God, showing himself that he is God" (2 Thessalonians 2:4). And he will be successful: "All who dwell on the earth will worship him, whose names have not been written in the Book of Life" (Revelation 13:8).

He Will Be a Cruel Leader

This ruler will "devour the whole earth, and trample it and break it in pieces" (Daniel 7:23). He will spare no one in his quest for world domination. Believers will be absent from the earth due to the Rapture when the Antichrist's wrath reaches its peak, but he will persecute those who seek to follow Christ during the Tribulation. Many who become Christians during the Tribulation will be martyred for their faith. Most others will simply be worn down (the literal meaning of "persecute" in this context) by the Antichrist's relentless persecution and oppression of their faith. In much the same way that Hitler drove Jews to madness in the concentration camps, so believers will be worn down by the cruelty of the Antichrist.

THE PROFILE OF THE COMING WORLD RULER

We are given enough information about this evil world leader to piece together a profile of his life and work for the few years he will be on the world stage.

His Inconspicuous Profile

We have evidence relating to his political, national, spiritual, and "providential" life.

1. Politically

Revelation 13:1 pictures the beast "rising up out of the sea"—the sea being a picture of the masses of humanity on planet earth (see a similar reference to "the waters" in Revelation 17:15). So the Antichrist does not burst on the scene. He rises slowly out of the Gentile nations of the earth, the nations of the revived Roman Empire in Europe, and gradually assumes power.

2. Nationally

The Bible doesn't tell us the nationality of the Antichrist. Some have thought he would be a Jew since he makes a treaty with the Jewish people (Daniel 9:27), but that is not a necessity. His charisma and cunning will allow him to forge political treaties and alliances with anyone. The best we can say is that he will come from among the ten rulers of the revived Roman Empire (the ten toes of Nebuchadnezzar's image).

3. Spiritually

His spiritual origin and empowerment is from "the bottomless pit" (Revelation 11:7). In short, the Antichrist comes from hell. The true Christ came from heaven, empowered by the Holy Spirit. The Antichrist comes from hell, empowered by Satan.

4. Providentially

Though this man seems to run amok, wreaking havoc on the world stage, he is on a leash that is tethered firmly in heaven. Note the words of Revelation 13:5: "And he was given a mouth speaking great things and blasphemies, and he was given authority to continue for forty-two months." Who gives him this authority to speak and to rule? God Almighty does.

It might seem that God is looking the other way during the period that the Antichrist rules over earth, but nothing could be further from the truth. Like every person who has ever lived, the Antichrist has nothing that did not come from God—and that includes permission to carry out his evil deeds. God does not give up control over His creation or His plans, and no one can wrest it from Him.

THE PROGRAM OF THE COMING WORLD RULER

Keep Revelation 13:2–3 in mind as we talk about the program of the Antichrist: "Now the beast which I saw was like a leopard, his feet were like the feet of a bear, his mouth like the mouth of a lion.

The Dragon gave him his power, his throne, and great authority. And I saw one of his heads that had been mortally wounded, and his deadly wound was healed. And all the world marveled and followed the beast."

The world is going to be looking for someone who can bring peace and stability to the Middle East. Remember that the majority of the world's petroleum reserves are there, plus the ongoing tensions between Israel and her neighbors. The Antichrist will come on the scene and be the savior. He will make a treaty with Israel on behalf of the nations. For three and one-half years there will be peace in the Middle East—until the Antichrist breaks the treaty and begins to persecute Israel.

At that point the Antichrist will be assassinated—I believe he will be shot in the head—but by the power of Satan, he will come back to life in a veiled counterfeit of the resurrection of Jesus Christ. This prophecy reminds me of the day president John F. Kennedy was assassinated in Dallas, Texas, where I was a seminary student at the time. Can you imagine what the world would have thought if, in just a matter of hours, he had risen from the dead and began to speak? Imagine the reaction on the world stage when the Antichrist does just that!

Whether his death and resurrection is real or feigned, the world will throw their support to one as powerful as he. His lieutenant, the biblical False Prophet (Revelation 16:13; 19:20; 20:10), will establish a form of registration that causes all to receive "the mark of the beast" (Revelation 16:2; 19:20). Those who receive the mark will be able to buy and sell while those who refuse will suffer starvation.

The Antichrist will set himself up as the one to be worshipped in the temple of the Jews in Jerusalem, thus beginning his fullfledged attack upon Israel. Before he carries out that mission, Jesus Christ returns from heaven with His army of the saints who were raptured seven years earlier. The Antichrist is defeated, the Jews are saved, unbelievers from all history are judged, and the kingdom of God is established upon earth for a thousand years (Revelation 20:1–3).

If you think this sounds impossible, read this very possible–sounding description by Gary Frazier:

Somewhere at this very moment, there may be a young man growing to maturity. He is in all likelihood, a brooding, thoughtful young man. Inside his heart there is this hellish rage. He boils like a cauldron of molten steel. He hates God.

He despises Jesus Christ. He detests the Church. In his mind, there is taking the shape of this dream of conquest. He presents himself as a friend of Christ in the church. Yet beneath his veneer of civility is a Trojan horse. He will, once empowered, pour all hell loose on this world. We ask ourselves, "Can this world produce such a person?" Hitler was a little boy one time. Stalin was once a lad. Nero was a child. And the tenderness of childhood will be shaped by the devil into the terror of the Antichrist.[2]

This person could be alive today as a child or young man—or a mature adult waiting to step into his appointed role. But that does not mean we will be here when he rules. The Church of Jesus Christ (all true believers) will have been removed at the Rapture when his reign of terror begins. Therefore, Christians are not looking for the coming of Antichrist but the coming of Christ! Here's an acrostic version of what it means to focus on Jesus instead of the Judas who is to come:

A : We abhor the Antichrist, we adore the Christ.

B : We blame the Antichrist, we believe in the Christ.

C : We curse the Antichrist, we confess the Christ.

D : We despise the Antichrist, we desire Christ.

E : We explain the Antichrist, we exalt the Christ.

F : We fear the Antichrist, we fellowship with Christ.

G : We glare at the Antichrist, we gaze at Christ.

H : We hate the Antichrist, we honor Christ.

I : We investigate the Antichrist, we insist on Christ.

J : We judge the Antichrist, we are judged by Christ.

K : We know about the Antichrist, but we know Christ.

L : We loathe the Antichrist, but we love Christ.

M: We minimize the Antichrist, we magnify Christ.

N : We nullify the Antichrist, we need Christ.

O : We oppose the Antichrist, we obey Christ.

P : We put down the Antichrist, we praise Christ.

Q : We question the Antichrist, we quote Christ.

R : We reject the Antichrist, we revere Christ.

S : We survey the Antichrist, we serve Christ.

T : We test the Antichrist, we trust Christ.

U : We unmask the Antichrist, we uplift Christ.

V : We vilify the Antichrist, we verify the Christ.

W: We warn against the Antichrist, we worship the Christ.

Y : We yawn at the Antichrist, we yearn for the Christ.

Z : We zone out the Antichrist, we zero in on Christ.

That's a playful look at a serious subject. We do not fear the Antichrist, and that is not just because we will be absent during His rule. Instead we fear (adore and revere) the King of Kings who is coming to defeat him and save God's chosen people, the Jews, from annihilation. The Book of Revelation is not about the revelation (appearing) of the Antichrist, but the Christ (Revelation 1:1). Knees may bow temporarily to the Antichrist, but when he becomes a defeated foe, the prophecy of Philippians 2:10–11 will be fulfilled: "That at the name of Jesus every knee should bow, of those in heaven, and of those on earth, and of those under the earth, and that every tongue should confess that Jesus Christ is Lord, to the glory of God the Father."

How much better to bow before Him now in praise and adoration!

Notes:

1. Charles Colson, *Kingdoms in Conflict* (Grand Rapids: Zondervan, copublished William Morrow, 1987), 129–130.

2. Gary Frazier, *Signs of the Coming of Christ* (Arlington: Discovery Ministries, 1998), 149.

1. Read 1 John 2:18–23.

   a. What is the implication of "you have heard" in verse 18? (How widespread was the Church's understanding of the Antichrist?)

   b. What is the difference between "the Antichrist" (is coming) and "many antichrists" (have come)? (verse 18)

   c. What did "the antichrists" do that identified them to John? (verse 19)

   d. What were the antichrists teaching that was indicative of their nature? (verse 22; see also 1 John 4:3)

   e. What doctrine is essential to Christianity? (verses 22–23)

   f. What will "the" Antichrist do in the future that is consistent with verses 22–23? (See 2 Thessalonians 2:4.)

2. Explain what John means in 1 John 4:3 about the "spirit of the Antichrist" that is "now already in the world."

   a. How does that change your perspective when you hear a person state that Jesus Christ is not the Son of God?

   b. Who is the ultimate "spirit of the Antichrist" when it comes to lying about Christ? (John 8:44)

DID YOU KNOW?

When president Ronald Reagan and his wife, Nancy, left the White House, they moved to a home that had been purchased for them in Bel Air, California. The address was 666 St. Cloud Road. Upon discovering the street number of the house, the Reagans immediately filed a request with the city to have the address number changed to 668—a request which was granted. This request had less to do with biblical conviction than general superstition on the part of the former president and first lady. But it is evidence of the general dislike of many for the number of "the man of sin" (2 Thessalonians 2:3) in Scripture.[3]

3. Laurie Becklund, "The Reagans: First Family Easing Into Private Life," *Los Angeles Times*, Nov. 19, 1988.

THE MARK OF THE BEAST

Revelation 13:1-18

In this lesson we learn about the satanic activity of the Antichrist and the False Prophet during the Tribulation.

OUTLINE

If a well-known political leader today suddenly began manifesting miraculous powers—signs and wonders—he would receive instant acclaim. During the Tribulation, Satan will give such power to the Antichrist and False Prophet to induce the world to worship them instead of God.

I. **The Mark Is Originated by Satan**

II. **The Mark Is Ordered by the Antichrist**

III. **The Mark Is Orchestrated by the False Prophet**
   A. The Description of the False Prophet
   B. The Deeds of the False Prophet
   C. The Deception of the False Prophet
   D. The Demand of the False Prophet
   E. The Doom of the False Prophet and His Followers

OVERVIEW

October 7, 2011, marked the anniversary of the barcode. The Universal Product Code barcode we use today was invented by an engineer at IBM and first used at a supermarket in Troy, Ohio, in 1974.

While the barcode is not going away, a new identification system—RFID (Radio Frequency IDentification)—is becoming even more widespread. It is a tiny microchip that is used to keep track of products in shipment, the movement of people (via a chip on a name or ID tag), even animals. RFID chips are everywhere—and usually unseen because of their tiny size. And the technology is now available to implant the chips, about the size of a grain of rice, under human skin. Their first use is to implant them under the skin of emergency workers, soldiers, and others to make identification possible as a last resort.

While fascinating, this technology is frightening at the same time, especially to those who have read Revelation 13—a chapter detailing some of the policies of the Antichrist during the Tribulation. We are already seeing a gradual erosion of privacy in our day; and during the Tribulation, citizens will have none. When we look at where technology is taking us, we can only stand in awe of the biblical prophecies made 1,900 years ago depicting these same events. God knows the beginning and the end, seeing past, present, and future as one (Isaiah 46:9-10). The Mark of the Beast, the subject of this lesson, is a prime example of how biblical prophecy will be fulfilled with today's technology.

I am often asked whether Christians, who will be raptured from the earth before the Tribulation, need to be concerned about these developments. We know the events of Revelation 13 take place in the second half of the seven-year Tribulation, or three-and-one-half years after the Rapture of the Church. We also know that the Rapture is imminent—that it could happen at any moment. No other biblical prophecy needs to be fulfilled before the Rapture can occur. So if the Rapture could happen today, then we could be just three or four years away from the events described in Revelation 13. But those events will not happen suddenly. There will be a gradual buildup to those events. And we are living in a time when the technology is developing and the sweeping power of government is growing to the extent that we could begin to see signs of the nearness of the Tribulation events taking place. I truly believe we are living in the shadows of Tribulation events.

Revelation 13 introduces us to the methods for population control the Antichrist will use in the second half of the Tribulation, one of them being a "mark" affixed to the hand or forehead of every individual on earth.

THE MARK IS ORIGINATED BY SATAN (REVELATION 13:2)

We are told in verse 2 that it is "the dragon" which gives "the beast" (the Antichrist) his power. The reference to Satan as "the dragon" comes from the previous chapter, Revelation 12:9, which depicts "the great Dragon" being cast out of heaven along with the rebellious angels who were allied with him. It is obvious in Revelation 12 that the Dragon is Satan. And in Revelation 13, John continues by saying it is the Dragon who empowers the Beast (the Antichrist).

It is Satan's desire to be worshipped that we see also in the Antichrist. In Isaiah 14:12-14 we find Satan saying, "I will be like the Most High" (verse 14). And when Satan tempted Jesus in the wilderness, he offered Jesus "all the kingdoms of the world" if Jesus would "fall down and worship [him]" (Matthew 4:8-9). It is Satan's long-standing desire to be worshipped "like the Most High," and it is no surprise that we have seen an increase in Satan worship in our day. And his primary goal during the Tribulation will be to deflect worship away from the true and living God to his (Satan's) representative on earth, the Antichrist.

Satan is a counterfeiter, a copycat. We'll see that just as God is a Trinity, Satan has his own trinity: himself, the Antichrist, and the False Prophet. Just as the Holy Spirit brings glory to Jesus Christ, so the False Prophet will bring glory to the Antichrist. The Mark of the Beast is a way to force people to worship someone out of fear.

THE MARK IS ORDERED BY THE ANTICHRIST (REVELATION 13:1-10)

John saw the Beast rising up out of the sea. The Beast is a composite of the four animals seen by Daniel in his prophecy of the end times. They represented Babylon, Medo-Persia, Greece, and Rome. The Beast has seven heads and 10 horns and represents the ruler of the revived Roman Empire, the Antichrist himself. He will be an international leader, uniting people from all races and all regions of the world. No human could do that alone, but with Satan working behind the scenes, it will happen.

The Antichrist's activities are detailed in verses 3-10, activities that are consistent with Satan's career—especially the Antichrist's blasphemous words against God. Satan's main mission in life is to make God look bad so people will not worship Him. And the Antichrist will take up that blasphemous task during his time on earth with the intent to turn people away from God to worship him.

He also makes war against the saints—those who profess faith in Christ during the Tribulation. He exercises power over "every tribe, tongue, and nation" (verse 7). And he is successful: "All who dwell on the earth will worship him"—all, that is, "whose names have not been written in the Book of Life of the Lamb slain from the foundation of the world" (verse 8). A frightening world is coming shortly.

THE MARK IS ORCHESTRATED BY THE FALSE PROPHET (REVELATION 13:11-18)

The mark is originated with Satan and ordered by the Antichrist, but it is orchestrated by the False Prophet—the second beast of Revelation 13. He is the one who executes the plan to put the Mark of the Beast on the population of planet earth.

The Description of the False Prophet (Revelation 13:11-12)

John notes that this second beast looks like a lamb but speaks like a dragon. That is, he appears meek and mild but, in reality, is bent on destruction. Again, Satan is all about counterfeiting. Jesus was "the Lamb of God who takes away the sin of the world" (John 1:29), so Satan makes the False Prophet into a false lamb. But this lamb is really a wolf in sheep's clothing, a demonized man exercising authority and power in the name of the Antichrist. He has miraculous powers by which he amazes and deceives the residents of planet earth (verses 13-14).

Though Christians will not be around to witness these miracles, we must beware of False Prophets today who are "ravenous wolves" in sheep's clothing (Matthew 7:15). Many could be named, but Jim Jones (The Peoples Temple) is a good example—a preacher who began his ministry based on Scripture but ultimately led hundreds of people to their deaths by suicide in Guyana. This tragic case of satanic deception ended in the deaths of hundreds of hopeful, but deceived, people.

The Deeds of the False Prophet
(Revelation 13:13)

I fear some Christians underestimate the power of our enemy. He gives the False Prophet power to work miracles—"great signs" —like making "fire come down from heaven on the earth in the sight of men." Satan is not God's peer or equal. But he is definitely powerful and can create "signs" that look equivalent to what God has done. Again, his expertise is counterfeiting.

The reason the False Prophet calls down fire from heaven is probably a reference to Malachi 4:5-6 which says that before the coming of the Messiah, Elijah will appear. And Elijah is the only Old Testament prophet to have called down fire from heaven. The False Prophet will be attempting to convince people he is Elijah— the forerunner of the Lord who will return. It is a deceitful attempt to give an air of legitimacy to his presence.

The Deception of the False Prophet
(Revelation 13:14-15)

The False Prophet's miracles have their intended effect: he convinces people to build "an image to the beast"—a giant image in honor of the Antichrist (verse 14). I believe the Antichrist then sets this image in the rebuilt Jewish temple in Jerusalem, in the Holy of Holies, thus fulfilling the prophecy of Daniel 12:11 (also in Daniel 9:27 and 11:31) concerning "the abomination of desolation." This prophecy of Daniel was fulfilled as a foreshadowing by Antiochus Epiphanes who set up a statue of the Greek god Zeus in the Holy of Holies and sacrificed a pig on the temple altar. These acts would have indeed been an abomination to any God-fearing Jew of the day. And the Antichrist will perform similar acts with the help of the False Prophet.

Jesus also made reference to this coming abomination in Matthew 24:15-16, 21. This act marks the beginning of the second half of the Tribulation (see the 1,290 days, or three-and-one-half years mentioned in Daniel 12:11). Following this event, Jesus said, "there will be great tribulation, such as has not been since the beginning of the world until this time" (Matthew 24:21).

At the beginning of the Tribulation, the Antichrist will make a covenant with Israel to protect her against her enemies. But he breaks the covenant at the midpoint of the Tribulation and turns against Israel by desecrating her temple and Holy of Holies. He defiles everything the Jews hold holy and turns his full fury upon Israel to destroy her. Paul says that the Antichrist will "sit as God in the temple of God, showing himself that he is God" (2 Thessalonians 2:4). At that moment, the diabolical trinity of Satan, the Antichrist, and the False Prophet have fulfilled their desire of receiving worship as God.

And here is a truly diabolical part: The False Prophet is able to cause the image of the Antichrist to speak (Revelation 13:15). There is no magic or deceit here. It is pure demonic power at work according to the testimony of 2 Thessalonians 2:9: "The coming of the lawless one is according to the working of Satan, with all power, signs, and lying wonders." Satan has the power to make an inanimate object like an image appear to come to life. It is another example of the dark power that will characterize the Tribulation period—especially the second half.

The Demand of the False Prophet
(Revelation 13:16-18)

Once the Antichrist and False Prophet's power have been displayed, they are ready to demand the acceptance of the Mark of the Beast "on their right hand or on their foreheads."

Again, counterfeiting is seen. In Revelation 7:3 the servants of God are sealed on their foreheads to set them apart from those not belonging to Him. These are the 144,000 Jewish witnesses who serve as evangelists during the Tribulation period. The seal is to protect them before certain judgments are released on the earth. The Antichrist's seal is for the same purpose: protection. By receiving his mark, people will be able to buy and sell and engage in commerce. Without it, they will become targets of the Antichrist. The RFID microchip already mentioned is a possible way for this to take place.

The Doom of the False Prophet
and His Followers (Revelation 19:19-20)

In spite of the power and control the Antichrist exercises during the Tribulation, his doom is sealed. We turn forward in Revelation to chapter 19 for the details. There we find that "these two [the Beast and the False Prophet] were cast alive into the lake of fire burning with brimstone" (verse 20).

And those who took the Mark of the Beast and worshipped his image did not fare well either. Revelation 16:1-2 details "a foul and loathsome sore" that came upon them. Revelation 14:9-11 says they will "drink of the wine of the wrath of God" and "shall be tormented with fire and brimstone in the presence of the holy angels and in the presence of the Lamb . . . forever and ever." While it may appear that those who take the Mark of the Beast are simply doing what they have to do to protect themselves and their families, they are judged for identifying with the satanic evil of the Antichrist.

What is the Mark of the Beast? Revelation 13:18 says, "Let him who has understanding calculate the number of the beast, for it is the number of a man. His number is 666." For 1,900 years people have wanted to know what 666 represents, who it points to. People are afraid of the number. We don't want it in our address or phone number.

Perhaps the best thing to remember is that the number seven in Scripture is the number of completeness —the divine number. Six, therefore, is an incomplete number, a number that falls short of God's completeness. And human beings certainly fall short of God's completeness due to sin. That may be what 666 represents: incomplete man rebelling against God.

What about those who refuse to take the Mark of the Beast? Revelation 20:4 identifies them as having been "beheaded for their witness to Jesus and for the word of God," for not worshipping the Beast or his image and not receiving the mark of the beast. "And they lived and reigned with Christ for a thousand years." They are resurrected and rule with Christ during the Millennium.

If you are a Christian today, you will never face the decision of whether to receive the Mark of the Beast or not. You will be in heaven with Christ during the Tribulation. But what would you do if you were faced with such a decision—a decision to swear allegiance to a godless ruler or maintain your allegiance to Christ? We have examples in Scripture of people faced with that choice: Daniel's three friends, Shadrach, Meshach, and Abed-Nego. They refused to worship the king of Babylon and were sorely tested—but God preserved them. They didn't know He would. They were willing to die as faithful Jews (Daniel 3).

That should be our stance today as well. Whether we are tested with ridicule, embarrassment, financial reversal, or even the threat of death—may God give us grace to stay true to the One who has given His all to save us for all eternity.

APPLICATION

1. Read Isaiah 14:12-14.

   a. Where was Satan (Lucifer) before being consigned to earth? (verse 12a)

   b. Describe the five prideful assertions Lucifer made that resulted in his downfall: (verses 13-14)

      1) I will _____

      2) I will _____

      3) I will _____

      4) I will _____

      5) I will _____

   c. Which of the five most clearly parallels the intention of the Antichrist during the Tribulation?

2. Read Matthew 7:15-20.

   a. What does Jesus warn His followers about in this passage? (verse 15)

b. Why does Jesus make this warning? (Is it possible that something can appear legitimate to us when it really isn't?)

c. How does Paul affirm this possibility in 2 Corinthians 11:13-15?

d. How do the men in Paul's day parallel the activity of the False Prophet during the Tribulation?

e. What does the term "ravenous wolves" in Matthew 7:15 signify to you? (How serious is the intent of False Prophets?)

f. How does Jesus say a False Prophet can be detected? (verse 16)

g. Why are miracles not always the only "fruit" that must be checked? (Revelation 13:13-14)

h. What other kinds of "fruit" should one look for? (Galatians 5:22-23)

3. Read Daniel 3:16-18.

   a. What were the three Hebrew men convinced God was able to do? (verse 17)

   b. Why is it important to decide on our convictions before pressure arises in our life?

DID YOU KNOW?

RFID (Radio Frequency IDentification) tags, like a barcode, require a reader to pull data stored on the RFID microchip. Because the information is transmitted wirelessly, RFID chips have an advantage over barcodes in that they can be read at a distance. RFID tags are currently used to track livestock (chips in ear tags), monitor individuals coming in and out of facilities (employees wearing ID badges with embedded chips), inventory control (chips embedded in clothing and on pallets of products in shipment), transportation payments (cars going through toll booths, passengers boarding buses, subways, and trains), timing of individuals and vehicles in sport races, tracking international travel via passport chips, and many other uses. Human implants of RFID chips have been in progress since 1998.

THE MARRIAGE SUPPER OF THE LAMB

Revelation 19:1-10

In this lesson we get a glimpse of the wedding and Marriage Supper of the Lamb.

You will find more in-depth information on this lesson in the book *Escape the Coming Night*, chapter 17, pages 217-222.

OUTLINE

With all the tumultuous and dark events taking place in the last few years of the Tribulation, the reader of Revelation longs for relief—a ray of celebration in the midst of judgment. It comes at the end of the Tribulation when heaven rejoices over God's victory and the marriage of His Son.

I.   **The Celebration in Heaven**
    A. The Hallelujah for the Salvation of God
    B. The Hallelujah for the Severity of God
    C. The Hallelujah for the Sovereignty of God
    D. The Hallelujah for the Supremacy of God

II. **The Ceremony**
    A. The Sacred Wedding
    B. The Supper Meal

W ith this lesson and our study of Revelation 19, we make a sudden turn in the "tone" of what we have studied thus far. Chapter 19 stands in sharp contrast to the content of the previous 18 chapters. The destruction of Babylon, the capital of the Antichrist's world empire, marks the end of the Great Tribulation. The horrors, which have filled the earth through the judgments God has poured out and through the demonically orchestrated actions of the Beast, have all been stilled. Darkness gives way to light, and sobbing is about to give way to song. The most anticipated event in history is about to take place—the Second Coming of Jesus Christ. That event forms the bridge between the gory days of the Great Tribulation and the glory days of the Millennial Kingdom.

The first ten verses of chapter 19 describe two events that take place in heaven at the end of the Tribulation: a celebration and a ceremony—both involving the Bride of Christ, the Church.

THE CELEBRATION IN HEAVEN

The multitude in heaven says, "Alleluia!" in praise to the Lord for what has been revealed about Him throughout the Great Tribulation. "Alleluia" is the Greek version of the Hebrew *Hallelujah*, a word which meant "praise ye the Lord." It is found only four times in the New Testament while occurring often in the Old—usually translated into English as "Praise the Lord!"

The Hallelujah for the Salvation of God

Some of the words in Handel's great "Hallelujah Chorus" come from the first six verses of Revelation 19. Indeed, some have called this section of Scripture the New Testament's "Hallelujah Chorus." God is praised in heaven for one simple reason. Those praising God are there because God provided their redemption. God has personally saved every person who makes it from earth to heaven, and He is worthy to be praised for that reason.

The Hallelujah for the Severity of God

Why would anyone rejoice and praise God for His severity? It is because of how and against whom His severity was directed. The destruction of Babylon, the world-controlling religious and economic system, has just occurred. Looking down from heaven, the saints see that these anti-God systems of thought and practice have been destroyed and eliminated from earth. It is for that reason they rejoice. They know God's judgments are "true and righteous" and that He judged the "great harlot who corrupted the earth with her fornication" (19:2). His severity also brought about vengeance for those who were martyred by the Beast.

The smoke from the destruction of Babylon going up "forever and ever" (19:3) is evidence that, even in the face of judgment, those at enmity with God do not repent and change their minds. I am continually surprised, as I study the Book of Revelation, at the hardness of heart of the impenitent sinner. No matter what judgment God brings or what mercy He extends, the carnal sinner continues to rebel against God. God's judgment is praiseworthy because it is just.

> *So long as the Godhead is to endure and so long as the believers are to reign with Him in glory, so long must the wrath of God be poured upon those who know not God and obey not the Gospel of our Lord Jesus Christ. There is not the shadow of evidence in the Bible that the lake of fire will ever turn one heart toward God or cause one guilty sinner to relax in the slightest the enmity against God that characterizes the carnal mind.*
>
> *Dr. John Walvoord*

The Hallelujah for the Sovereignty of God

The key word in this third reason for rejoicing in heaven is "Amen" (19:4). This is a word of sacred ratification in Scripture, a word of sealing and of affirmation. When the 24 elders and the four cherubim say, "Amen! Alleluia!" they are giving consent and affirmation to an act of judgment that they know to be righteous and true. "Amen" and "Hallelujah" are not English words; rather they are transliterations of Hebrew words which are pronounced the same in every language. Believers from around the world who do not speak each other's language can establish instant fellowship and communion when they share an "Amen" and "Hallelujah" together. When heaven and earth agree by saying "Amen!" to God's acts, it is an affirmation of His sovereignty over all things.

The Hallelujah for the Supremacy of God

Verses 5 and 6, while the last of the words of praise offered to God, are actually a prelude to the wedding ceremony that is about to take place. They are both a conclusion to the acknowledgement that God has acted sovereignly in judgment upon sin on earth and an introduction to His sovereignty in saving a multitude from earth who will be united forever with His Son. It is like the music we listen to in the hour just before a wedding ceremony takes place, music which speaks of the greatness of the ceremony we are about to witness.

THE CEREMONY

An invitation is issued in verses 7-9. This is the event which all true believers should be anticipating more than any other—the moment in which they become one with their Savior, where the Bride of Christ and the Head of the Church are united.

Understanding the rituals of a Jewish wedding ceremony will help us understand the Marriage Supper of the Lamb, the wedding and the ceremony. There were three major steps in the pattern of marriage in the ancient Near East. Step one was the legal marriage, often originated and arranged by the parents of the bride and bridegroom. This involved the payment of a dowry and resulted in a legal marriage. Often it was accomplished solely by the parents without the bride and groom having met one another. Secondly, after the legal marriage, the groom (with his friends) would go to the house of the bride and "claim" the bride for himself, taking her back to his own house. The final stage of the wedding was the bridal procession followed by a marriage feast which would often last for several days.

Following this outline, we can see clear parallels in our relationship with the Lord. First, the legal marriage takes place at the time of our conversion to Christ—positionally we are already united with Him by faith. As the Bride of Christ, we are now awaiting the time when the groom will come to claim us for Himself and take us back to His own mansion which He has been preparing for us (John 14:2). Finally, the Marriage Supper of the Lamb takes place after we have been taken to be with the Groom.

When reading the account in Revelation of the marriage of the lamb, it is important to understand the relative importance of the groom to the bride. In modern weddings, all attention is focused on the bride, but in Oriental weddings the opposite was true. The groom was the central figure. The Lamb of God is the central figure in this marriage and marriage supper.

The Sacred Wedding

This refers to the second of the three steps outlined above in the ancient pattern for marriage, the coming of the Bridegroom to claim the Bride for his own. This is fulfilled, of course, at the Rapture of the Church. We anticipate the day when the Lord Jesus Christ will return for us, His bride, and take us to be with Himself. Prior to that event, though legally married, we are still in an engagement period, as Paul expressed in 2 Corinthians 11:2: "I have betrothed you to one husband, that I may present you as a chaste virgin to Christ." The Church at present is engaged to Christ, waiting on the day when He returns to claim us as His own.

Scripture does not tell us exactly when the marriage takes place in heaven, but it would appear to happen in this order: Rapture, Judgment Seat of Christ, marriage ceremony, Second Coming of Christ. The Rapture and Second Coming are the "bookends" on the seven-year Tribulation period, so the marriage ceremony takes place during that time.We know the marriage ceremony takes place after the Judgment Seat of Christ because of Revelations 19:7 and 8: The Bride has made herself ready, and she is arrayed in clean and bright linen which is the righteous acts of the saints.We know from 1 Corinthians 3 that the unrighteous works of the saints are burned up with fire at the Judgment Seat of Christ so that only righteous deeds remain. If the Church appears clothed in fine linen, which is her righteous deeds, it is because she has already passed before the Judgment Seat of Christ.

The most important person at the wedding is the Bridegroom, who is here referred to as "the Lamb" (:). Why does Christ come to this wedding ceremony as "the Lamb" instead of any of the 700 other titles by which He is referred to in Scripture? From our perspective as the Bride of Christ, I think I know why He comes to the wedding as "the Lamb." I think it is because we fell in love with the Lamb.While we honor Him as King, Creator, Servant, and all the other titles of which He deserves, we were saved by Him as the Lamb, the Lamb of God who takes away the sin of the world.

> *The wedding gown will be made by the master Designer, and it symbolizes the righteous deeds done by the Bride on earth . . . The lavishness or drabness of that wedding gown will be determined by a report on the deeds performed on earth in the Spirit, not in the flesh. How we use the gifts God gave us on earth will decide the way we are presented to the Bridegroom when He comes.Will we be dressed shabbily or lavishly?*
>
> *David Jeremiah*
> **Escape the Coming Night**

The Supper Meal

The marriage supper is mentioned in verse 9. There is some detail which we need to note concerning the location of the supper. While the wedding ceremony itself appears to take place in heaven, the marriage supper seems to be held on earth.

After the wedding ceremony, the Lord returns to earth with His Bride at the Second Coming. Since verse 9 says, "Blessed are those who are called to the marriage supper," it is obvious that there are more than just the Bride and Bridegroom at the supper. The Bridegroom is Christ and the Bride is the Church. So who are the others? John the Baptist gives us a clue in John 3 when he speaks of the "friend" of the groom, who in that passage has to be Israel. Therefore, it would appear that the Marriage Supper of the Lamb is held on earth so that the redeemed of Israel, who have gone through the Tribulation and survived the persecutions of the Antichrist, may attend and rejoice at the marriage supper. So the Marriage Supper of the Lamb will be a magnificent redemptive meal celebrating the uniting of Jews and Gentiles into one body, married to the Head of the Body, Jesus Christ. The fact that it takes place on earth is a prelude to the thousand years the Bridegroom and Bride will spend reigning over the earth during the Millennium. The time of our preparation and purification is almost over. The day of the marriage ceremony is close at hand.

The Old Testament story of Abraham's preparation of a bride for Isaac is instructive regarding our marriage to the Lamb (Genesis 24). Abraham is a picture of God the Father, Isaac a picture of Christ, Abraham's servant Eleazar a picture of the Holy Spirit, and Rebekah a picture of the Christian. Just as Abraham sent Eleazar to a foreign land to seek out a bride for Isaac, so the Holy Spirit has been moving throughout the earth seeking out the Bride of Christ. Every time someone is saved, the Bride's identity becomes more complete. As Isaac went to meet Rebekah when he saw Eleazar approaching, so Christ descends to meet His Bride. As Eleazar and Isaac took Rebekah to meet Abraham, so the Church will be taken before the Father in order for the ceremony and the supper to take place.

The Father has sent the Spirit into the world to call out a bride for His only Son. The Bride (the Church) has been legally transferred from her former domain to the domain of the Father; her citizenship is in heaven. Meanwhile, the Son is preparing a heavenly home for His Bride. He will return to take His Bride to Himself, and join with her in a ceremony in heaven and a feast on earth among the friends of the Son. What a beautiful picture! If the Bridegroom comes tonight to meet His Bride and take her to meet the Father, will you be among those taken? Don't let another day go by without being sure you are part of the Bride of the Lamb.

1. Read Ephesians 5:22-33.

    a. What is the "great mystery" that Paul wrote about to the Ephesian church? (Verse 32)

    b. What is Christ's ultimate goal for the Church? (Verse 27)

    c. How does Romans 8:29 parallel this purpose?

    d. How does Romans 8:28 fit into God's ultimate purpose for the Church? How do "all things" ultimately result in the church being "holy and without blemish"? (Ephesians 5:27)

    e. How is the Word of God able to cleanse believers from sin? 2 Timothy 3:16; Hebrews 4:12)

    f. What is the ultimate source of our purity before Christ? (1 John 1:7)

i. What parallel does Paul draw between Christ and husbands? (Ephesians 5:28-29)

2. Read 1 Corinthians 3:9-17.

   a. Rather than a bride, what metaphors does Paul use in this passage to refer to the Church? (Verse 9)

   b. Regarding the "building" metaphor, what does he say about the "foundation" (verses 10-11) and the "construction" (verses 12-13) process? (1 Corinthians 3:13-15)

   c. How will the Christian's "works" ("righteous acts"; Revelation 19:8) be tested? What are the two possible outcomes of the test?

DID YOU KNOW?

Unfortunately, the Hebrew word "hallelujah" is a biblical word that has become a cultural colloquialism in the modern world. In the Old Testament, "hallelujah" is usually translated "Praise the Lord!" (Psalm111:1; 112:1; 113:1). That's because it is made up of two Hebrew words: *halelu* (a plural, imperative verb) and yah, a shortened form of "Yahweh," the personal and intimate name for the God of Israel. Combining the two results in *halelu yah*, or "hallelujah" in English. In the New Testament, the Greek word *allelouia* is simply a transliteration of the Hebrew halelu yah (as in Revelation 19:1, 3, 6).

ARMING FOR ARMAGEDDON

Revelation 16:13–16; Daniel 11:36–45

*In this lesson we learn about earth's final war—
and how it ends.*

OUTLINE

The word "Armageddon" is used in modern cultures to describe
doomsday-type events—or even a "meeting with the boss." Many
people don't know it is the biblical name for earth's final great
battle—when Israel is saved from annihilation and the rebellious
nations of earth are defeated.

I.   **The Preparation for the Battle of Armageddon**

II. **The Place of the Battle of Armageddon**

III. **The Purpose of the Battle of Armageddon**
   A. To Finish His Judgment Upon Israel
   B. To Finalize His Judgment Upon the Nations That Have
      Persecuted Israel
   C. To Formally Judge All the Nations That Have Rejected Him

IV. **The Perspective of the Battle of Armageddon**

V.   **The Participants in the Battle of Armageddon**
   A. The Deal Between Israel and Antichrist
   B. The Demand That Everyone Worship the Antichrist
   C. The Decision to Fight Against the Antichrist
   D. The Disturbing News From the East
   E. The Descending Lord From the Heavens

A merica is no stranger to war. Since the beginning of our
nation, we have experienced a major war about every
twenty-five years beginning with the Revolutionary War,
the War of 1812, the Civil War, The Spanish-American War, World
Wars I and II, the Korean War, the Vietnam War, the Persian Gulf War,
and the wars in Afghanistan and Iraq. Hardly any generation has
been able to live their whole life without sending their young to war.

The Bible says there is going to be a final war one day on this
earth. That war, called Armageddon, will signal the coming down
of the curtain on modern civilization. And preparation for that war
is under way in our world at this very moment. The only thing
blocking the players in that war from moving onto the stage of battle
is the Rapture—the transfer of the Church of Jesus Christ to heaven.
Following that event, the final war—the Battle of Armageddon—
will take place.

THE PREPARATION FOR THE
BATTLE OF ARMAGEDDON

The Battle of Armageddon begins in heaven and descends to
earth with the casting out of Satan (Revelation 12:9–13). Satan is the
"prince of the power of the air" (Ephesians 2:2)—his dominion is
the heavenly region surrounding planet earth. But in the middle of
the seven-year Tribulation, he will be cast out of that domain to
earth where he will begin to persecute "the woman who gave birth
to the male Child" (Revelation 12:13). The "woman" is not Mary,
Jesus' mother, but Israel—the one through whom Jesus Christ came
into this world. Satan's goal will be to destroy Israel before the
return of Christ to establish His kingdom on earth.

Satan will have two human helpers: the Beast and the False
Prophet (Revelation 16:13). These three form an unholy trinity of
persecution against God's chosen people during the Tribulation.
And it is that reign of terror against Israel that will lead the world
to the Battle of Armageddon.

THE PLACE OF THE BATTLE
OF ARMAGEDDON

Revelation 16:16 identifies Armageddon as a place in the Holy
Land. "Armageddon" is a Hebrew word made up of two smaller
words: "har" (mountain) and "Megiddo" (slaughter). So Armageddon

is "mountain of slaughter." I once stood on a hill overlooking the vast Plain of Megiddo in northern Israel—twenty miles southeast of Haifa and fifty miles north of Jerusalem. In 1799 the French conqueror Napoleon stood at Megiddo and declared, "All the armies of the world could maneuver their forces on this vast plain. There is no place in the whole world more suited for war than this. It is the most natural battleground on the whole earth."[1]

The Battle of Armageddon will not be fought only at Megiddo—it will spill over into all of Israel and even other parts of the world. Joel says there will be fighting in "the Valley of Jehoshaphat" which is east of Jerusalem (Joel 3:2). Isaiah says the sword will fall on Edom which was south of the Dead Sea (Isaiah 34:5). And Zechariah refers to Jerusalem as being part of the stage of battle (Zechariah 12:2).

Revelation 14:20 says blood will flow "up to the horses' bridles, for one thousand six hundred furlongs." That distance in furlongs is about 200 miles—exactly the distance from one end of Israel to the other. The "horses' bridles" reference is an ancient one probably referring to quantity. In other words, a great deal of blood is going to be spilled in the Battle of Armageddon.

THE PURPOSE OF THE BATTLE OF ARMAGEDDON

Why would God allow such a blood-bath to take place on earth? There are three biblical reasons.

To Finish God's Judgment Upon Israel

For all the sympathy it is easy to feel toward Israel during this period when she is being attacked by others, we have to remember that she is still living in rebellion toward God. Even the reestablishment of the nation in 1948 was more a Zionist cultural, political movement than a spiritual one. Israel to this day has not embraced her Messiah, and judgment will fall upon her for that reason. It is that judgment that will cause many Jews during the Tribulation to turn to God and accept the Messiah they rejected (Zechariah 12:10).

To Finalize His Judgment Upon the Nations That Have Persecuted Israel

As God allows the nations of the world to inflict judgment upon Israel, He will be inflicting judgment on them: "I will also gather all nations, and bring them down to the Valley of Jehoshaphat; and I will enter into judgment with them there" (Joel 3:2).

In the first lesson in this study guide, we noted God's promise to "curse those who curse [Abraham and his descendants]" (Genesis 12:3). And that is why these nations of the world will be judged during the wars that make up Armageddon.

To Formally Judge All the Nations That Have Rejected Him

Revelation 19:15 says that God will "tread the winepress of the fierceness of the wrath of Almighty God." Not only will the nations be judged because they have attacked Israel but also because they have rejected God and His Son, the Lord Jesus Christ. Psalm 2 pictures the Lord in heaven laughing at the "kings of the earth" who "take counsel together" against God and His Anointed. But they will be judged for their rejection of Him.

THE PERSPECTIVE OF THE BATTLE OF ARMAGEDDON

Let's reset the stage for this end-time conflagration: The Church of Jesus Christ is raptured to heaven, which marks the beginning of the seven-year Tribulation period. The ruler of the European nations, the Antichrist, makes a peace treaty with Israel ensuring her safety from the surrounding Arab nations—a time when Israel is living in "unwalled villages" (Ezekiel 38:11). During this time the coalition of nations from "the north" (Russia, Iran, and others) attacks Israel but is stopped and defeated by God in the Battle of Gog and Magog. This is not the Battle of Armageddon—these two battles need to be kept separate:

Gog and Magog	Armageddon
• Russia, Iran, and at least five other nations	• All the nations of the world
• Invaders come from the north	• Invaders come from all directions
• Purpose is to take Israel's wealth and land	• Purpose is to annihilate the Jews and fight against Christ and His armies as they return to earth
• Russia will be the leader	• The Antichrist will be the leader
• Invaders are defeated by earthquake and disease	• Invaders are defeated by Christ
• Those killed limited to land of Israel	• Armies killed all over the earth
• The dead will be buried	• Dead will be consumed by birds
• Not the final battle on earth	• The final war before the Millennium begins [2]

THE PARTICIPANTS IN THE BATTLE OF ARMAGEDDON

There are five major stages in the Battle of Armageddon—beginning with the treaty between Israel and the Antichrist.

The Deal Between Israel and the Antichrist

Daniel 9:27 is the verse that tells us about the "covenant" (treaty) the Antichrist makes with Israel—a seven-year peace-protection pledge. From his position of power in the revived Roman Empire (Europe)—and his apparent resurrection from an assassination—he begins to accumulate power and "speak blasphemies against the God of gods" (Daniel 11:36). The "god" of his own strength and power is the only god he worships (Daniel 11:37–39).

With this power he convinces Israel to enter into a treaty that will protect Israel from the growing storm of threats against her in the world—specifically from her Arab neighbors.

The Demand That Everyone Worship the Antichrist

If you think the world is looking for answers today to problems like global climate change, food shortages, gas prices, and warring nations, it is only going to be worse in the future. Life in the future is not going to get easier, it's going to get harder. When the Antichrist rises to the stage of power, people will be eager to submit to him. His seeming supernatural abilities will cause people to see him as the savior of mankind.

But after signing the peace treaty with Israel, he makes a mistake: he demands that people worship him under threat of death (Revelation 13:15). Some of the earth's peoples rebel at this extension of the Antichrist's power, which sets the stage for the next movement.

The Decision to Fight Against the Antichrist

Daniel 11:40 says that the "king of the South" and "the king of the North" will attack the Antichrist. If you consider that many nations of the world have strong religious heritages—especially Muslim nations—it's not difficult to see how some would resist, even refuse, the idea of worshipping the Antichrist as a god. So they decide to move against him and remove him from power.

Daniel's prophecy describes a great army from Africa, including not only Egypt, but other countries of the continent. The army, probably numbering in the millions, will attack the Middle East from the south. And at the same time, Russia and other armies from the north will mobilize another powerful military force. Even though Russia may have lost a lot of its people and military four years earlier in the Battle of Gog and Magog, they will apparently have recovered enough to begin to recoup their losses and get involved in this battle again. And so what happens at the beginning is, the Antichrist is all puffed up with his power, demanding the worship of the world; and here are the armies of the North and the South coming and saying, "We're going to take this guy out. We'll not have him do this to us."[3]

The Disturbing News From the East

As the Antichrist is resisting the armies from the South and the North, "news from the east and the north shall trouble him; therefore he shall go out with great fury to destroy and annihilate many" (Daniel 11:44). Suddenly the Antichrist is being attacked from all different directions. Revelation 16:12 pictures a great army coming from the east over a dried-up River Euphrates. The number of that army coming from the east is 200 million (Revelation 9:16). Many Bible students stumble at the thought of a 200-million-man army. But it would not be difficult, given the population of China alone, for a coalition of countries from the east (Asia) to field an army of 200 million soldiers.

So the Antichrist is facing armies coming at him from all directions. But there is a supernatural component to this: "For they are the spirits of demons, performing signs, which go out to the kings of the earth of the whole world, to gather them to the battle of that great day of God Almighty" (Revelation 16:14).

The Descending Lord From the Heavens

These armies are moving toward Israel under the inspiration of Satan himself. Satan's goal, of course, is to gather all the armies of the world to attack Israel and destroy her for good. The problem is that, while everyone has been checking north, south, east and west, they have forgotten to check "up." If they had, they would have seen the Lord Jesus Christ Himself descending with His armies from heaven:

Now I saw heaven opened, and behold, a white horse. And He who sat on him was called Faithful and True, and in righteousness He judges and makes war. His eyes were like a flame of fire, and on His head were many crowns. He had a name written that no one knew except Himself. He was clothed with a robe dipped in blood, and His name is called The Word of God. And the armies in heaven, clothed in fine linen, white and clean, followed Him on white horses. Now out of His mouth goes a sharp sword, that with it He should strike the nations. And He Himself will rule them with a rod of iron. He Himself treads the winepress of the fierceness and wrath of Almighty God. And He has on His robe and on His thigh a name written: KING OF KINGS AND LORD OF LORDS (Revelation 19:11–16).

Israel suddenly gets reinforcements from the sky—reinforcements no one had anticipated. And it changes the entire battle scene. The armies that return with Jesus Christ are made up of saints—all true believers who were raptured off the earth prior to the Tribulation—and angels. If you are a Christian, you will be part of this army that descends from heaven with Christ.

1. Descending With All His Saints

Several verses in Scripture refer to the appearance of God with His saints at the end of time: Zechariah 14:5; 1 Thessalonians 3:13; 2 Thessalonians 1:10; Jude 1:14. Think of the number of saints this represents—all the faithful from the beginning of time who were resurrected at the Rapture—including those who were alive on earth at the Rapture! That's how they got to heaven.

It is a finite number, but one that is too large to consider estimating. At the least, it is a number that will make the gathered armies of earth look puny in scope. The column of saints coming behind Christ on His white horse (Revelation 19:11) will be the most awe-inspiring sight in all of human history and will no doubt strike fear in the hearts of all on earth.

2. Descending With All His Angels

Along with the saints from the ages will come the heavenly hosts—the angels of heaven: "When the Son of Man comes in His glory, and all the holy angels with Him, then He will sit on the throne of His glory" (Matthew 25:31; see also 2 Thessalonians 1:7).

Christians are going to fight side-by-side with angels! But wait—there is no record in Scripture of us lifting a single finger in the fight. Rather, it is the "sharp sword" going "out of [Christ's] mouth" with which He "strike[s] the nations" (Revelation 19:15). That "sharp sword" is not a literal sword. Because it comes out of His mouth, it is a metaphor for the words of judgment He will speak, words that will signal the end of the rebellious armies of earth. He will speak and it will be over.

So what is our purpose on that day? It is the same as we have seen in other settings where God intervenes: so that His glory might be revealed to us. Second Thessalonians 1:10 says that on that day He will be "glorified in His saints and . . . admired among all those who believe." All the saints of the ages—that great "cloud of witnesses" (Hebrews 12:1)—will witness Christ in all His glory pronounce judgment on those who oppose God and His people, the Jews.

In a day when Israel has no earthly allies by her side, the only true ally she has ever had, her own Messiah, saves her from destruction. If you want to see the greatest battle in history ended with a word, make sure you are among the armies of heaven who return with Christ and witness His judgment.

Notes:

1. J. Vernon McGee, *Through the Bible, Vol. 3* (Nashville: Thomas Nelson, 1982), 513.

2. Adapted from Carl G. Johnson, *Prophecy Made Plain for Times Like This* (Chicago: Moody Press, 1972), 169–170.

3. John Walvoord with Mark Hitchcock, *Armageddon, Oil and Terror* (Carol Stream: Tyndale House, 2007), 174.

1. From Revelation 16, describe the events that take place prior to and at Armageddon.

   a. By whose authority are the events leading to Armageddon ordered? (verse 1)

   b. What do the seven bowls in verse 1 represent?

   c. What did the first angel pour out on those worshipping the Antichrist? (verse 2)

   d. What happened to the oceans as a result of the second angel's bowl? (verse 3)

   e. What ironic interpretation did the third angel give to the effects of the third bowl judgment? (verses 4–6)

   f. Who does the voice of the "altar" represent in verse 7? (Revelation 6:9. Why would this group agree with the angel's statement in verses 5–6?)

   g. What was the content of the fourth bowl judgment? (verse 8)

   h. What was the content of the fifth angel's bowl? (verse 10)

i. What did the sixth angel's bowl accomplish? (verse 12)

j. How do we know that the Antichrist and his False Prophet will be demonically possessed? (verses 13–14)

k. What happens when the seventh angel pours out his bowl? (verses 17–21)

l. Compare the words coming from the temple (verse 17) with the words spoken in John 19:30? How are they two different aspects of the same conclusion?

2. From what you have learned so far in this study guide, what is the only way to avoid the calamitous events described in Revelation 16?

DID YOU KNOW?

We speak of the "battle" of Armageddon as if it was a onetime event—a single battle. In reality, it is more of a war or a campaign. The Greek word translated "battle" in the Book of Revelation and other places in the New Testament occurs a total of eighteen times and is translated "wars" or "war" as often as battle. A war or military campaign is made up of many battles and such will be the case with the Battle of Armageddon. It will involve many battles fought throughout the land of Israel over a three-and-one-half year period of time. The Battle of Armageddon usually refers to the culminating event in which Christ defeats the gathered foes of God—the last battle in the lengthy war.

THE RETURN OF THE KING

Revelation 19:11–21

In this lesson we study the details of Christ's victory in earth's greatest battle.

OUTLINE

Planet earth's most amazing day is yet to come: The largest massing of armies in world history will turn their faces skyward to see Jesus Christ descending from the clouds with His own armies. By the word of His mouth, He will pronounce judgment upon all who rebel against God.

I. **The Anticipation of Christ**

II. **The Advent of Christ**
   A. The Designation of Christ
   B. The Description of Christ

III. **The Armies of Christ**

IV. **The Authority of Christ**

V. **The Avenging of Christ**
   A. The Fowls of Heaven
   B. The Foes of Heaven

VI. **The Application of Christ's Second Coming**
   A. We Should Refrain From Judging Others
   B. We Should Remember the Lord's Table
   C. We Can Relate to One Another in Love
   D. We Can Recommit Ourselves to Ministry
   E. We Must Refuse to Neglect the Church
   F. We Must Reach the Lost for Jesus Christ

The first and second comings of Christ are both important—but they are very different. Note the following comparisons:

Christ's First Coming	Christ's Second Coming
• Clothed in swaddling clothes	• Clothed in a robe dipped in blood
• Surrounded by cattle and common people	• Surrounded by armies of saints and angels
• The door of the inn was closed to Him	• The door of heaven is opened for Him
• His voice was the cry of a baby	• His voice is like the sound of many waters
• The Lamb of God for salvation	• The Lion of the Tribe of Judah for judgment

In this lesson on the prophetic future of planet earth, we examine the climax of all prophetic Scriptures: the return of Jesus Christ to earth to reign as King of Kings and Lord of Lords.

THE ANTICIPATION OF CHRIST

Next to faith, the Second Coming of Christ is the most dominant subject in the New Testament. For every one time the first Advent of Christ is mentioned, the Second Coming is mentioned eight times. Jesus Himself is recorded as mentioning His Second Coming twenty-one times. There are 333 prophecies about Christ in the Bible, but only 109 were fulfilled at His first coming, leaving 224 to be fulfilled at the Second Coming.

Christ's Second Coming is mentioned throughout the Bible. Zechariah the prophet mentions it (Zechariah 14:4), angels mention it (Acts 1:11), Jesus declared He would return (Matthew 24:17, 29), the apostle John confirmed it (Revelation 1:7)—just to mention a few.

Never let anyone tell you that the Second Coming of Christ is immaterial to the message of the Bible. It is a central doctrine and must be taught as part of the whole counsel of God.

THE ADVENT OF CHRIST

Revelation 19 is the central prophetic passage in Scripture on the actual return of Jesus Christ to earth. When He returns, it will be to the same place from which He ascended: the Mount of Olives in Jerusalem (Acts 1:10–12).

The Designation of Christ

There are three different names given to Christ in Revelation 19: "Faithful and True" (verse 11), "The Word of God" (verse 13), and "King of Kings and Lord of Lords" (verse 16). Those names represent Him and His ministry: His unchanging nature from eternity past (Hebrews 13:8), His incarnation as the living Word (John 1:14), and His future role as ruler of God's kingdom (Luke 1:32).

The Description of Christ

Revelation 19:12–13 gives a magnificent description of Christ: eyes like flaming fire and a head on which were many crowns, clothed in a robe dipped in blood. Eyes of fire mean there will be no posturing or pretending in His presence. His eyes will burn away all pretense and see men's hearts as they really are. The multiple crowns speak of His ultimate kingship over all the so-called kings of the earth, making Him worthy for every knee to bow before Him (Philippians 2:10). The robe dipped in blood reminds us that He is the "Lamb who was slain before the foundation of the world" (Revelation 13:8).

I believe throughout eternity the representation of the Lord Jesus Christ we will see is as the Lamb of God. We will see His nail-scarred palms and His spear-wounded side and be reminded for all eternity that He is the only reason we are there. We will have the same response that the apostle John had when he said, "Behold! The Lamb of God who takes away the sin of the world!" (John 1:29)

THE ARMIES OF CHRIST

The armies who return with Christ are all the saints of the ages—having been in heaven since the Rapture, seven years prior—and the angels. In verse 14 we learn how we will appear: "clothed in fine linen, white and clean, [following] Him on white horses." Soldiers normally don't wear white into battle but in this case, it's okay because we are not actually going to enter into combat. It is the word of His judgment (the "sharp sword" going out of His mouth) that carries the day. Jude 14–15 gives the most detailed explanation of the reasons for this judgment: "to convict all who are ungodly among them of their ungodly deeds . . . and of all the harsh things which ungodly sinners have spoken against Him."

When Christ returns, it is primarily for judgment. Remember that most of the people on the earth at this time have rejected the 144,000 evangelists (Revelation 14:1) and two witnesses (Revelation 11:3–14) that God sends during the Tribulation. In other words, they are deserving of judgment. God never sends judgment without first having sent a warning or an opportunity to believe. But a time will come when judgment is no longer delayed.

THE AUTHORITY OF CHRIST

When Christ returns, the parts of Isaiah 9:6–7 that were not fulfilled in His first coming will be fulfilled: He will assume His place on the throne of His forefather David and "of the increase of His government and peace there will be no end." There was never a time in His first coming that "the government [was] upon His shoulder." The Old Testament prophets saw truth in their prophetic vision—in this case, the complete picture of God's Messiah—but they did not always see the timing. They did not see the gap of time between His first and second coming.

When He returns, He will rule with the authority given to the throne of David in Israel. He will "strike the nations" and "rule them with a rod of iron" (verse 15). And there will be no end to His authority, government, and the resulting peace.

THE AVENGING OF CHRIST

The Battle of Armageddon is where justice is meted out upon the ungodly on this earth (verses 17–21).

The Fowls of Heaven

An angel in heaven calls to "all the birds that fly in the midst of heaven" for them to "gather together for the supper of the great God" —meaning for them to consume the flesh of the armies killed in the last battle when Christ returns (verses 17–18). These are essentially vultures that come to pick over the bones of the dead after the massive destruction of humanity.

This supper to which the vultures are called is the second supper described in Revelation 19, the first being the Marriage Supper of the Lamb (verse 9)—the celebration of the union between Christ and His Church. I strongly suggest making reservations now for the Marriage Supper of the Lamb rather than "the supper of the great God."

The Foes of Heaven

Even though the Antichrist's doom is sealed, he still gathers the armies of earth to fight against the returning Christ.

1. The Futility of Fighting Against God

Verse 19 presents something almost unbelievable: "And I saw the beast, the kings of the earth, and their armies, gathered together to make war against Him who sat on the horse and against His army."

The Antichrist is obviously a very intelligent human being, but this is not a smart move on his part: going up against the Son of God in battle. This is the ultimate act of rebellion of Satan, the one inspiring the Antichrist—a last-ditch effort to inspire humanity to shake its collective fist in the face of God. This attempt, like all others, will be futile.

2. The Fatality of the Beast and the False Prophet

The Beast and the False Prophet were captured and "were cast alive into the lake of fire burning with brimstone" (verse 20). The "lake of fire" is, of course, eternal hell. Satan, the one who inspired them, will end up there as well, but a thousand years later (Revelation 20:7–10). During the Millennium Satan is confined but set free near the end. He foments a rebellion against Christ but is judged and confined to the lake of fire along with the Beast and the False Prophet where they will be "tormented day and night forever and ever" (Revelation 20:10).

It's a sad fact that nobody talks about hell anymore—especially preachers. But there's more in the Bible about hell than about heaven. It will be a shame someday for people to be facing an eternity in hell because the reality of that place was never mentioned in the churches they attended for years. Preachers shouldn't preach on hell every Sunday, but they definitely should preach on it when and where it occurs in the biblical text. To avoid it is to deny people the truth. The fact that Satan, the Antichrist, and the False Prophet all spend eternity there makes it an unsavory place for people to go. We ought to be honest about the reality of hell so at least people know what their future holds if they choose to reject Jesus Christ.

3. The Finality of Christ's Victory Over Rebellion

With Satan bound for a thousand years, Christ will rule an earthly kingdom of peace, righteousness, and justice. He will sit on the throne and oversee the turning of implements of war into implements of agriculture and peace (Isaiah 2:4; Micah 4:3). There will be no war during the Millennium and only a short rebellion at the end when Satan is loosed from his chains in preparation for his judgment. The human race will experience for the first time what it means to live under the rule and reign of God Himself.

THE APPLICATION OF CHRIST'S SECOND COMING

We have covered a lot of prophetic ground in this study guide on what is going on in the world—and will be going on in the future. I have six observations on how we should live in light of the coming end-time events.

We Should Refrain From Judging Others

In 1 Corinthians 4:5 the apostle Paul wrote, "Therefore judge nothing before the time, until the Lord comes, who will both bring to light the hidden things of darkness and reveal the counsels of the hearts. Then each one's praise will come from God."

In other words, when Christ returns He will set all the accounts right; He will judge what needs to be judged—for believers before the Millennium (1 Corinthians 3:11–15) and unbelievers at the end of the Millennium (Revelation 20:11–15). But don't misunderstand this point: "Don't judge" doesn't mean we don't call "sin" sin. It doesn't mean we don't identify evil and wickedness and immorality where we see it and take a stand against it. It means we should not jump to conclusions and condemn people when we ourselves might be guilty of the same things (Matthew 7:3–5).

We Should Remember the Lord's Table

Second, we should be faithful in "[proclaiming] the Lord's death until He comes" (1 Corinthians 11:26) by participation in the Lord's Table. When we gather as a corporate body for Communion, we look back at the death of Christ and remind ourselves of why He died. But we do that knowing it is a temporary remembrance: We do it "until He comes." So the Lord's Table keeps us mindful of Christ's death and His Second Coming at the same time.

We Can Relate to One Another in Love

First Thessalonians 3:12–13 says we should "increase and abound in love to one another and to all" so that our hearts might be "blameless . . . at the coming of our Lord Jesus Christ with all His saints."

If you recall from previous lessons, all the saints of God will be united together in the army of Christ when we return with Him at the end of the Tribulation period when He executes judgment upon the ungodly nations of the earth. Since we are going to be united then, shouldn't we live united today? That is, shouldn't we be exercising love toward one another ("and to all") in all we do now? Since we are going to spend eternity together, it behooves us to begin to live that way in our earthly relationships. There is no convincing argument for why we shouldn't.

We Can Recommit Ourselves to Ministry

This next one is primarily an exhortation to preachers like myself: "I charge you . . . Preach the word! Be ready in season and out of season. Convince, rebuke, exhort, with all longsuffering and teaching" (2 Timothy 4:1-2). Preachers of the Word are to be faithful, saying exactly what God says—especially as the time nears for the return of Christ. And that applies to any who minister the Word in Christ's stead until He returns: Bible study leaders, Sunday school teachers, personal counselors, campus ministry discipleship leaders, and Bible teachers in Christian schools. As the time draws near for Christ's return, people's opportunities to respond to the Gospel or obey the Word of God become fewer. We must speak the truth— in love, yes (Ephesians 4:15)—but always the truth.

We Must Refuse to Neglect the Church

This exhortation is for every Christian, not just those who preach or teach the Word: "Not forsaking the assembling of ourselves together, as is the manner of some, but exhorting one another, and so much the more as you see the Day approaching" (Hebrews 10:25).

"The Day" is the day of Christ's coming for His Church. And as things begin to cycle downward in the last days, it will take being an active part of the body of Christ to "stir up love and good works" (verse 24) as things get more and more dark. Church attendance is not just for contributing money and singing worship songs. It is to be encouraged by the Word and the Spirit and by one another! It's not easy to maintain a faithful Christian walk in today's world, and the possibility is good that it is going to get more difficult in the future.

In light of that reality, it is amazing that church attendance is falling. Churches that used to meet together on Sunday morning and evening and Wednesday night now only meet on Sunday morning. And many Christians think nothing of skipping a Sunday morning service for the slightest of reasons. Don't be one of those. Be found in the midst of a corporate body of believers as often as possible to give and receive encouragement.

We Must Reach the Lost for Jesus Christ

Finally, we must take to heart the words of Jude: "And on some have compassion, making a distinction; but others save with fear, pulling them out of the fire" (verses 22–23).

The end times are nearer today than they were yesterday. That means we have less time than before to extend the saving Gospel of Christ to those who will end up with Satan, the Antichrist, and the False Prophet in the lake of fire if they don't embrace it. And how will they hear without someone to tell them (Romans 10:14)? May you and I redouble our desire and effort to pull them "out of the fire."

And may our prayer be, with the Apostle John, "Even so, come, Lord Jesus!" (Revelation 22:20)

1. Describe the setting of Luke 4:16–22. (When was it in Jesus'
   ministry; to whom was He speaking?)

   a. Compare the text of Isaiah with Jesus' quotation of it in Luke
      4:18–19. Find the key element from Isaiah that Jesus did not
      quote. (Hint: It's in Isaiah 61:2.)

   b. Why didn't Jesus quote that part of Isaiah's prophecy at
      this time?

   c. Separate the elements of Isaiah 61:1–2 into two categories: those
      pertaining to Christ's first coming and His second coming.

      Christ's First Coming   **Christ's Second Coming**

d. How does Revelation 19:11–21 fulfill Isaiah 61:2b?

2. Read Isaiah 11:1–10.

a. Divide the elements of this passage into those pertaining to the first and second comings of Christ (list them by verses).

Christ's First Coming   **Christ's Second Coming**

b. How do the prophets' visions parallel the way God sees time? That is, does God see past, present, and future separately or as one vision?

3. What promise is given in Revelation 22:7 concerning the prophecies of the Book of Revelation?

George Frideric Handel's most well-known composition is *Messiah*, written in 1741, of which the most beloved section is the "Hallelujah Chorus." That chorus is based on three Scripture passages from Revelation that describe the Second Coming of Christ:

- 11:15 "The kingdoms of this world have become the kingdoms of our Lord and of His Christ, and He shall reign forever and ever!"

- 19:6 "Alleluia! For the Lord God Omnipotent reigns!"

- 19:16 "And He has on His robe and on His thigh a name written: KING OF KINGS AND LORD OF LORDS."

WHAT ON EARTH IS THE MILLENNIUM?

Revelation 20:1–10

*In this lesson we learn about
Christ's future thousand-year rule over earth.*

OUTLINE

Imagine a TV nature show where you see a lion sneaking up on a bale of hay instead of an antelope. During the Millennium, peace will rule the earth—including the animals! Christ's kingdom will be characterized by peace, prosperity, purity, prolonged life, and personal joy.

I. Three Perspectives on the Millennium
A. Post-Millennialism
B. A-Millennialism
C. Pre-Millennialism

II. Four Purposes of the Millennium
A. To Reward the People of God
B. To Respond to the Prophets' Predictions
C. To Receive the Answer to the Disciples' Prayer
D. To Reemphasize Man's Depravity and the Necessity of Christ's Death

III. Five Profiles of the Millennium
A. It Will Be a Time of Peace
B. It Will Be a Time of Prosperity
C. It Will Be a Time of Purity
D. It Will Be a Time of Prolonged Life
E. It Will Be a Time of Personal Joy

OVERVIEW

Almost everyone knows the lyrics to Isaac Watts' famous hymn, "Joy to the World," but few people realize that it is not really a Christmas hymn. A quick look at the lyrics will explain why:

Joy to the world, the Lord is come!
Let earth receive her King;
Let every heart prepare Him room,
And heaven and nature sing . . . .
[Did mankind receive the king when Jesus was born at Bethlehem?]

Joy to the earth, the Savior reigns!
Let men their songs employ;
While fields and floods, rocks, hills and plains,
Repeat the sounding joy . . . .
[Has nature rejoiced at the coming of Christ?]

No more let sins and sorrows grow,
Nor thorns infest the ground;
He comes to make His blessing flow
Far as the curse is found . . . .
[Has the curse been lifted from the earth?]

He rules the world with truth and grace,
And makes the nations prove
The glories of His righteousness,
And wonders of His love . . . .
[Is Jesus ruling the nations of the world?]

The words of this great hymn more accurately describe the coming Millennium, the time when Christ will rule over the earth at His second coming, not His first. The Millennium will be a foretaste of the heavenly state that is to follow. Revelation 20:1–10 is the central passage in the Bible on the Millennium and will be our focus in this lesson.

"Millennium" is a Latin word made up of two words: *Mille* means "thousand," and *annum* means "years." Therefore, combining the two yields millennium, or a period of a thousand years. "Millennium" doesn't occur in our English Bibles, but the reference to a thousand-year period of time does—six times in Revelation 20:1–10. As we will see in this lesson, the Millennium is a period of one thousand years that begins with Christ's second coming to earth. He establishes His kingdom in Jerusalem and brings in a period of peace and justice on the earth.

Christians through the years have viewed the Millennium from three different perspectives.

THREE PERSPECTIVES ON THE MILLENNIUM

Few topics in Bible interpretation generate as much heat among Christians as does the Millennium because of the way one's view impacts other end-time events.

Post-Millennialism

The word "post," when used as a prefix, means "after." Therefore, Post-Millennialists believe that Christ's second coming will occur after the Millennium.

This view suggests that the church will saturate the world with the Gospel. Its impact on people and culture will be radical, transforming the earth into a place of peace and prosperity where the worship of God is universal. Christ will then return to inherit the peaceable kingdom that His Gospel has brought about.

Post-Millennialism was popular until World War I shattered the notion that mankind could ever bring about universal peace. This view has lost credibility since universal peace has been a rare commodity despite the spread of the Gospel.

A-Millennialism

The prefix "a" on a word acts to negate the meaning of the word (amoral means without morals). Therefore, A-Millennialism means there will be no literal Millennium, no thousand year period of time. The "thousand" in Revelation 20:1–10 is purely symbolic according to this view.

Proponents of this view believe the events described in Revelation 20:1–10 are happening now; they have been working themselves out in the church over the last 2,000 years. The church is reigning with Christ at present, this view holds. The peace and prosperity assigned to the Millennium is a spiritual peace and pros-perity, not a literal one.

Pre-Millennialism

The prefix "pre" obviously means "before." Pre-Millennialism, which I believe teaches that the return of Jesus Christ to earth will happen before the Millennial period, not after (Post-Millennialism). Christ will defeat the enemies of God (the Battle of Armageddon) and establish a thousand-year reign of peace and justice on earth.

Here's a simple diagram showing where the Millennium fits in God's plan:

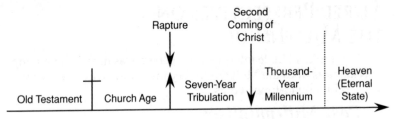

This diagram will be familiar to many as a diagram of Pre-Millennial eschatology (doctrine of the last things). After the Crucifixion, Christ returns in the air to remove His Church from the earth. Dead believers are resurrected, and living believers follow them into the air where they meet the Lord. The seven-year Tribulation ensues, concluded by the Battle of Armageddon where Christ returns to defeat the enemies of God. The second coming of Christ inaugurates the thousand-year reign of Christ, a time of universal peace on earth. At the conclusion of the Millennium, the Great White Throne judgment consigns the wicked, the devil, and his angels to the lake of fire. The earth is renovated, the New Jerusalem descends upon the earth, and the eternal state begins.

The Pre-Millennial view holds that all the promises made to Israel in the Old Testament are fulfilled, and believing Jews are returned to their homeland in Israel to serve their Messiah, Jesus Christ.

The Pre-Millennial view is the oldest interpretation of Revelation 20:1–10 in church history and is embraced by more evangelical Christians today than any other view of the Millennium.

FOUR PURPOSES OF THE MILLENNIUM

There are four purposes for the thousand-year period of time on earth, each supporting the necessity for a literal thousand-year period of time on earth.

To Reward the People of God

There are many promises in the Bible about rewards that are to be given to the people of God for their faithful service (Isaiah 40:10; Matthew 16:27; 25:34; Colossians 3:24; Revelation 22:12). A kingdom has been prepared, Jesus said, for those blessed of the Father as an inheritance (Matthew 25:34); and Paul said that Christians will receive the "reward of the inheritance" (Colossians 3:24).

This reward is different from the reward of the crowns. The Millennial kingdom is a reward by which we will reign and rule with Christ over the earth for a thousand years (Matthew 19:28; 1 Corinthians 6:2; Revelation 20:4). When Christ returns to earth, He will bring with Him the saints who have believed in Him. The twelve apostles will sit on twelve thrones "judging the twelve tribes of Israel" (Matthew 19:28). Our responsibilities in the Millennium will be based on our faithfulness in this life (Matthew 25:14–30).

Randy Alcorn has written these helpful words on this subject: "The idea of service as a reward is foreign to a lot of people who don't like their work, who only put up with their work until it's time to retire. We think that faithful service should be rewarded with a long vacation. But God offers us an opportunity very different from work: More responsibilities is His reward. Increased opportunities is His reward, greater abilities and resources and wisdom and empowerment. We will have sharper minds, stronger bodies, clearer purpose and unabated joy."[1]

To Respond to the Prophets' Predictions

The second purpose of the Millennium is to fulfill the words of the Old Testament prophets. Without the Millennium, the Old Testament Scriptures are left open-ended and unfulfilled. Here are just a few that are yet to be fulfilled:

- Psalm 72:11 Kings and nations must worship Christ.
- Isaiah 9:7 The Messiah's government must be established on David's throne.
- Isaiah 60:21 Israel must turn to righteousness and inherit her land forever.
- Zechariah 9:10 The nations must live in peace under Messiah's rule.
- Luke 1:32–33 Christ must rule over Israel as her Messiah in an unbroken rule.

Without the Millennium, these and many other prophecies would go unfulfilled. The focus of God's promises to Israel was that she was and is His chosen nation to be ruled over by the Prince of Peace. That has not happened yet, so it must happen in the future. Christ was rejected once by Israel (John 1:11), but He will ultimately be received by her (Zechariah 12:10). The kingdom that the apostles were looking for (Acts 1:6) will indeed come to pass for a thousand years in the Millennium.

To Receive the Answer to the Disciples' Prayer

Jesus taught His disciples to pray, "Your kingdom come. Your will be done on earth as it is in heaven" (Matthew 6:10). That prayer, prayed innumerable times through the centuries of church history, remains unanswered. With the Millennium will come the kingdom of God on earth—and the answer to the disciples' prayer.

To Reemphasize Man's Depravity and the Necessity of Christ's Death

Satan will be bound during the Millennium (Revelation 20:2–3). But the last phrase of Revelation 20:3 says he will be released for a "little while" at the end of the thousand years, at which time he will lead a rebellion against Christ, the king (Revelation 20:7–9). People forget that during the thousand years on earth, the righteous believers who enter the kingdom will bear children—but righteousness is not inherited. The sin nature of man will still be alive and well, and some will not submit to the rule of King Jesus then any more than they do now. Though with Satan being out of the picture for a thousand years, the sin nature of man will not be enticed as it is now. But when Satan is released, he will stir up rebellion against God just as he did in the Garden of Eden.

This experience will demonstrate that sin is man's fundamental problem—not the environment, training, education, influences, or genetics. At the end of the Millennium, at the Great White Throne Judgment, no one will be able to blame their environment. Even with Christ on the throne in a righteous world, some will still choose to rebel.

FIVE PROFILES OF THE MILLENNIUM

Following are five characteristics of the Millennium—what life will be like during the thousand years.

It Will Be a Time of Great Peace

It will take more than the United Nations to bring "peace on earth and good will toward men." Indeed, it will take God Himself. The Scriptures are full of predictions concerning the peace that one day will characterize planet earth. The famous words of Micah 4:3 are a well-known example:

"He shall judge between many peoples,
And rebuke strong nations afar off;

They shall beat their swords into plowshares,
And their spears into pruning hooks;
Nation shall not lift up sword against nation,
Neither shall they learn war anymore."

Isaiah 11:6–9 is another well-known passage that indicates there will be peace even in the animal kingdom and between man and the beasts of the field. There will be no armies, no military budgets, and no wars. What the United Nations has tried to do, Jesus will bring to pass.

It Will Be a Time of Prosperity

Everyone is seeking prosperity in this world, but the Millennium will be a time of prosperity like nothing ever seen before. Most of the promises given to Israel concerning future prosperity were given in agricultural terms because that was common in that day. But the same environment that will allow agriculture to abound will also support prosperity in other endeavors as well.

Consider the words of Ezekiel 34:26–27 as an example.

"I will make them and the places all around My hill a blessing; and I will cause showers to come down in their season; there shall be showers of blessing. Then the trees of the field shall yield their fruit, and the earth shall yield her increase. They shall be safe in their land; and they shall know that I am the Lord, when I have broken the bands of their yoke and delivered them from the hand of those who enslaved them."

Amos 9:13 says, "The plowman shall overtake the reaper," and Isaiah 35:1 says, "The desert shall rejoice and blossom as the rose."

Prosperity will cover the earth like the morning dew.

It Will Be a Time of Purity

Sin will be kept in check, and disobedience will be dealt with efficiently. Christ's rule will be righteous and His kingdom will be holy.

Isaiah 11:9 says, "The earth shall be full of the knowledge of the Lord as the waters cover the sea." And Zechariah 13:2 says, "I will cut off the names of the idols from the land, and they shall no longer be remembered. I will also cause the prophets and the unclean spirit to depart from the land."

An amazing thing will happen during the Millennium: Christ's presence will be known and felt all over the earth, and many will willingly respond to His rule in submission.

It Will Be a Time of Prolonged Life

We know that life spans were hundreds of years long before the Genesis flood and declined steadily thereafter. But in the Millennium, people will once again live long lives. In fact, a hundred-year-old person will be considered to be still a child (Isaiah 65:20). If a person 100 years old is viewed as a child, then it appears life spans will revert to pre-flood lengths: seven, eight, and nine hundred years long. Science has failed to produce a "Fountain of Youth," but the Millennium will restore longevity to all inhabitants of planet earth.

It Will Be a Time of Personal Joy

Because of the rule of a righteous King whose justice will keep life in balance around the world, many of the causes of heartache will be removed. The Millennium will be a time of unprecedented joy as a natural by-product of peace. Isaiah 14:7 says, "The whole earth is at rest and quiet; they break forth into singing."

The day is coming, as Paul wrote, when every knee will bow and every tongue will confess that Christ is Lord (Philippians 2:10–11)—and it is called the Millennium. If you want to live to see that day, you must begin today by bowing and confessing that Jesus is Lord.

Note:

1. Randy Alcorn, *Heaven* (Wheaton: Tyndale House Publishers, 2004), 226.

1. Read Isaiah 9:7.

   a. From whose throne would the coming Messiah rule over
   His kingdom?

   b. By what two standards would the Messiah's kingdom be
   ordered and established?

2. Read Isaiah 11:1-10.

   a. What will characterize the rule of the "Rod from the stem of
   Jesse as He rules and judges? (verse 2)

   b. What will He use as His benchmark for ruling—and what
   will He not use? (verses 3-4)

   c. Why is righteousness the defining trait that characterizes
   God's judgments and rule? (verses 4-5)

   d. Who is this descendant of Jesse? (Matthew 1:6, 16; Luke 3:23, 31)

3. What was the central message of John the Baptist and Jesus of Nazareth at the beginning of their ministries? (Matthew 3:2; 4:17, 23; 5:3, 10, 19-20).

a. What did Jesus teach His disciples to pray for? (Matthew 6:10)

b. What aspect of the millennial kingdom of Christ do you most anticipate in terms of its reversal of current conditions on earth?

DID YOU KNOW?

The English word "millennium" is derived from two Latin words: *mille* (thousand) and *annum* (year). Within the Christian tradition, three schools of interpretation have developed about the Millennium, or thousand-year rule of Christ mentioned in Revelation 20:1-6. Premillennialists take this reign literally, the "pre" referring to Christ's return being before the Millennium as taught in this study guide. Amillennialists believe the thousand years should be taken figuratively, not literally; that it refers to the present period in which Christ's victorious rule over Satan and death is experienced. And Postmillennialists believe the church creates a righteous reign on earth for a thousand years, following which Christ returns.

THE GREAT WHITE THRONE JUDGMENT

Revelation 20:11-15

*In this lesson we encounter the sobering
end for those without Christ.*

You will find more in-depth information on this lesson in
the book *Escape the Coming Night*, chapter 18, pages 234-239.

OUTLINE

Somewhere in the process of explaining the Gospel to a nonbeliever,
the following objection will be raised: "I could never believe in a
God who would send someone to hell." But as clearly as the Bible
teaches that God receives believers into heaven, so it teaches He
sends nonbelievers to hell.

I. **The Place of the Great White Throne Judgment**

II. **The Person at the Great White Throne Judgment**

III. **The People at the Great White Throne Judgment**

IV. **The Purpose of the Great White Throne Judgment**
   A. The Passing of the Sentence
   B. The Stipulations of the Sentence

V. **The Punishment at the Great White Throne Judgment**

Have you ever been to court to plead your case before a judge? I hope not. It is not a very enjoyable experience. The first time I went to court was a few years back after getting a traffic ticket. After a little investigation, I decided to go to court and plead my case to the judge. To make a long story short, I finally ended up paying for the ticket which is what I should have done in the first place. I discovered that the traffic court was not particularly interested in my well-reasoned arguments.

In this lesson we are going to learn about a courtroom experience far different than any on earth. As cumbersome and frustrating as it can be to go through some of our earthly court systems, many people would take a traffic court any day over the court described in Revelation 20:11-15, with one exception. The court John saw in his vision is characterized by absolute and total justice.

The Great White Throne Judgment is the final bar of justice in God's plan for the unsaved inhabitants of planet earth. Unlike earthly courtrooms, there will be a Judge but no jury, a prosecutor but no defender, and a sentence but no appeal. It is the place where sinners stand before a holy God to give an account of their sins. There is no more awesome scene presented to us in the Word of God in terms of the magnitude of its significance.

The Great White Throne Judgment is not the same as the Judgment Seat of Christ. These two judgments bring into focus two different resurrections mentioned in Revelation 20. Beginning with Christ's resurrection from the grave, the first resurrection includes the saved dead of this age who are raised at the Rapture, and seven years later those martyred during the Tribulation, and Old Testament saints who are raised at the end of the Tribulation. All of that is the first resurrection, or resurrection unto life. The second resurrection takes place at the end of the Millennium and includes "the rest of the dead [who] did not live again until the thousand years were finished" (20:5). This resurrection takes place a thousand years after the first resurrection and includes those dead spiritually as well as physically. This is the resurrection that leads to the Great White Throne Judgment, at which there will be no believers.

THE PLACE OF THE GREAT WHITE THRONE JUDGMENT

While we do not know where the Great White Throne Judgment takes place, we do know where it does not. It is not in heaven or on earth. It cannot take place on earth because at the appearance of the Lord, "the earth and the heaven fled away" (20:11). And it cannot take place in heaven because no sinner can enter into the presence of God in heaven. The only answer is that this judgment takes place somewhere between heaven and earth. Perhaps the name of the throne itself is more important than its location. "Great" speaks of the Infinite One who is the Judge; "White" speaks of divine holiness, purity, and justice; and "Throne" speaks of the majesty of the One who has the right to determine the destiny of His creation.

THE PERSON AT THE GREAT WHITE THRONE JUDGMENT

The Judge upon the Great White Throne is none other than the Lord Jesus Christ Himself. He said in John 5:22 and 27 that "the Father judges no one, but has committed all judgment to the Son . . . and has given Him authority to execute judgment also, because He is the Son of Man." Peter declared that "[Christ] . . . was ordained by God to be Judge of the living and the dead" (Acts 10:42). The spiritually "living" He will judge at the Judgment Seat of Christ, the spiritually "dead" at the Great White Throne. The One upon the throne is the very One who gave His life for the redemption of those He is about to judge. He must reject those who rejected Him and His plan for their salvation.

Consider this, you that are here present, that yet remain in an unregenerate state . . .
When God beholds the ineffable extremity of your case . . .
He will have no compassion upon you, He will not forbear the executions of His wrath, or in the least lighten His hand; there shall be no moderation or mercy, nor will God then at all stay His rough wind;
He will have no regard to your welfare, nor be at all careful lest you should suffer too much in any other sense, than only that you shall not suffer beyond what strict justice requires.

Jonathan Edwards

THE PEOPLE AT THE GREAT WHITE THRONE JUDGMENT

In verse 12, the phrase "great and small," describing those who stand before God and His throne, is very interesting. It is found often in the Old Testament and five times in Revelation. The phrase tells us that every class of person will be represented on that day. No position or standing in this world, or lack of it, will excuse one from judgment before God. God is not a respecter of persons. There is only one thing for which men will be judged on that day, and it is what they have done about Jesus Christ. If a person, be he great or small, has rejected Jesus Christ and has not believed on Him, he will appear before the Great White Throne. It is often alleged that the great and powerful fare better before the judges of our land than the small, but in that day all will be judged with equity.

THE PURPOSE OF THE GREAT WHITE THRONE JUDGMENT

The Passing of the Sentence

Verse 12 tells us that when all were gathered before the throne of God, "books were opened." There has been some confusion about the purpose of this judgment, some believing that its purpose is to decide whether a person is lost or saved. That is incorrect. Everyone appearing before the Great White Throne is lost on the basis of not placing his or her faith in Christ. This judgment is to judge the evil works of the unsaved. Men are judged from the "Book of Life" and other "books." Though we are not told specifically what the other "books" are, we have some indications from Scripture of what they might contain, that is, on what basis mankind will be judged at the Great White Throne.

1. The Book of Conscience

Romans 2:15 speaks of those "who show the work of the law written in their hearts, their conscience also bearing witness, and between themselves their thoughts accusing or else excusing them." This suggests that one day the human conscience may play a role in judging the nonbeliever: Did they violate their own conscience in the things they did? No person, saved or unsaved, can say that he has followed the dictates of conscience 100 percent of the time. And the conscience is not an infallible guide to what is right or wrong. But when the conscience is brazenly violated, it shows an attitude toward sin that may be brought to bear against the unbeliever.

2. The Book of Words

Matthew 12:36-37 says, "But I say to you that for every idle word men may speak, they will give account of it in the day of judgment. For by your words you will be justified, and by your words you will be condemned." Scientists tell us that no word we ever speak out loud is ultimately lost and that the sound waves continue on indefinitely, available to be recaptured someday. Whether that is true or not, it illustrates that once our words are spoken they can never be retrieved. They may act as the accusers of the unsaved one day at the Great White Throne Judgment. When excuses begin to be offered for past works, the Book of Words may be opened. By a man's own words, he may stand condemned before the Lord.

3. The Book of Secret Works

The apostle Paul taught that "God will judge the secrets of men by Jesus Christ" (Romans 2:16), and Solomon said, "For God will bring every work into judgment, including every secret thing, whether good or evil" (Ecclesiastes 12:14). D. L. Moody, the famous evangelist, used to say that if a camera were ever invented that could take a picture of the heart of man, the inventor would starve to death. No one would buy a camera that would expose the secret things of one's heart. But at the Great White Throne Judgment there will be no more secret things. Everything that men thought were secrets will be exposed before God. Those things which men thought would never be used against them because they were secrets will stand as testimonies against them.

4. The Book of Public Works

Paul speaks also of men "whose end will be according to their works" (2 Corinthians 11:15). Jesus said "the Son of Man will come in the glory of His Father with His angels, and then He will reward each according to his works" (Matthew 16:27). God will

> *They will die the second time. From the second death there is no resurrection. They will be sent out into the wide universe into the outer darkness. They will be wandering stars to whom the blackness of darkness is reserved forever. They will wander through this unlit darkness of eternity as derelicts of humanity, tossed upon an endless and shoreless sea; souls that have missed the purpose for which they were created—union and fellowship with God.*
>
> *Dr. I. M. Haldeman*

have a complete record of every moment of every person's life, not only their secret works but also their public works. Who a man is will be borne out by what he has done, how he has lived.

5. The Book of Life

The Book of Life is no doubt the most important of the books that will be opened. The Book of Life is mentioned a number of times in the Bible (e.g., Exodus 32:32-33; Psalm 69:28; Daniel 12:1; Philippians 4:3; Revelation 3:5; 13:8; 17:8; 21:27; 22:19). Many of those passages are in contexts dealing with believers, not unbelievers. This obviously raises the question of whether a Christian can have his name blotted out of the Book of Life. Some first century cultural background will aid our understanding of this question.

Cities in John's day had a city register which listed the names of every citizen. If a person committed crimes, or otherwise defiled his standing in the city, he could be called before a tribunal and his name removed from the city registry, literally blotted out. He would no longer be considered a citizen of that metropolis and would live from then on in anonymity or be forced to move elsewhere. I believe that concept forms the background for the Book of Life as John describes it. It is a book originally containing the name of every person ever born into this world. If that person dies having rejected God's offer of salvation, his name is blotted out of the Book of Life. It is a sobering thing to think about a person paging through God's Book of Life in vain looking for his name and not finding it.

William R. Newell, a great scholar and commentator on Revelation, said there are four things to be noted about the Book of Life:

1. It is the absence of one's name, not one's good works, that dooms a person.

2. Evil works are not the issue. Many of earth's greatest sinners' names are recorded in the Book of Life because they accepted God's offer of salvation.

3. Those whose names do not appear in the Book are cast into the lake of fire (20:15).

4. All names found in the Book were written before the Judgment Day. There is no record of names being recorded (decisions being made) on that day.[1]

The Stipulations of the Sentence

A final purpose we can mention for the Great White Throne Judgment is to determine degrees of punishment. It is a little-known fact among Bible students that there are degrees of punishment in hell. Jesus taught by a parable in Luke 12:47-48 that those who are given more will be held more accountable than those given less. We can only conclude that some will be held more accountable by God, and therefore punished more severely, than others. For example, a person who has continually rejected, time after time, a clear presentation of the Gospel will be held more accountable by God than someone who has never heard the Gospel clearly.

THE PUNISHMENT AT THE GREAT WHITE THRONE JUDGMENT

Both here, in verse 14, and in Matthew 25:41, 46, the concept of eternal punishment in hell is taught. It is not a popular doctrine, but it is a plain one in Scripture. Jesus spoke three words about hell for every one word He spoke about heaven. It was His compassion that prompted Him to warn men of that punishment to come if they did not accept God's salvation. Sometimes I wonder if the reason God does not allow believers to be present at the Great White Throne Judgment is that we would not be able to bear the looks of unsaved friends or relatives when they asked, "Why didn't you tell me?"

If there is someone you know whose name, as far as you know, will not be found in the Book of Life, won't you tell him soon about salvation in Jesus? Whether they choose Jesus is their responsibility, but whether they have the choice may be yours.

APPLICATION

1. What gave the psalmist gladness and hope as he approached death? (Psalm 16:9-11)

2. Though Job wasn't confident he would survive his ordeal of testing, what confidence did he have about his ultimate future? (Job 19:25-27)

3. Read Romans 2:12-16.

   a. How will people be judged by God—knowledge or actions? (Verses 12-13)

   b. What part of unbelievers' lives will Jesus Christ judge on "the day"? (Verse 16)

DID YOU KNOW?

The great hope of biblical revelation, compared to other ancient religions, is nowhere illustrated better than by the "Book of Life." This book is mentioned eight times in the New Testament (Philippians 4:3; Revelation 3:5; 13:8; 17:8; 20:12, 15; 21:27; 22:19) as the written record of those who will inherit eternal life through Christ. In stark contrast to the biblical Book of Life is the ancient Egyptian "The Book of the Dead." This book developed over many years in Egypt as a collection of descriptions and conceptions of the afterlife. Its primary purpose was to help the dead navigate expected obstacles encountered in the life after death.

Notes:

1. William R. Newell, *The Book of Revelation, 9th Edition* (Chicago: Moody Press, 1953), 334.

PURSUE YOUR REWARD UNTIL I COME

Selected Scriptures

In this lesson we learn about the rewards that await those who live a life of faithfulness to Christ.

OUTLINE

It's easy to grow weary of living sacrificially in this life, especially when surrounded by a culture that lives the opposite way. The antidote to such weariness is the biblical doctrine of rewards. Sacrifices made by faithful believers in this life will be rewarded many times over in eternity.

I. The Judgment of Believers' Works
A. This Is Not About God's Judgment of the Believer's Sin
B. This Is Not About a Believer's Judgment of Any Other Believer

II. The Rewards for Believers' Works
A. The Crown of the Victor
B. The Crown of Rejoicing
C. The Crown of Righteousness
D. The Crown of Life
E. The Crown of Glory

III. Four Applications
A. Reject the Misconceptions
B. Remember That the Lord Himself Is Our Chief Reward
C. Resist Doing Works Outwardly for a Reward
D. Reflect on the Ultimate Goal of Rewards

Rewards are part of God's plan for His people. Revelation 22:12 reminds us: "Behold, I am coming quickly, and My reward is with Me, to give every one according to his work."

THE JUDGMENT OF BELIEVERS' WORKS

Rewards are present everywhere in Scripture. Listen to some of these statements from the Word of God.

Psalm 58:11: "So that men will say, 'Surely there is a reward for the righteous; surely He is God who judges in the earth.'"

Psalm 62:12: "Also to You, O Lord, belongs mercy; for You render to each one according to his work."

In the New Testament, the Lord Jesus constantly talked to His disciples about the importance of rewards.

Mark 10:29–30 reads, "So Jesus answered and said, 'Assuredly, I say to you, there is no one who has left house or brothers or sisters or father or mother or wife or children or lands, for My sake and the gospel's, who shall not receive a hundredfold now in this time—houses and brothers and sisters and mothers and children and lands, with persecutions—and in the age to come, eternal life.'"

Matthew 5:12 says, "Rejoice and be exceedingly glad, for great is your reward in heaven, for so they persecuted the prophets who were before you."

The word *reward* comes from a couple of Hebrew and Greek words, and it means "payment for something done." In the New Testament, we find a well-defined system for the day when God rewards His people.

So if we are wondering, "What shall we do while we wait for the Lord to come back?" one of the things we ought to think about is what will take place after the Rapture. One of the events in heaven will be the Judgment Seat of Christ, or the "Bema Seat" of Christ. Everyone who is a Christian is going to be brought before that judgment seat—not to determine whether or not he goes into heaven (that will already be decided), but to be judged according to rewards earned.

In Romans 14:10 we read, "But why do you judge your brother? Or why do you show contempt for your brother? For we shall all stand before the judgment seat of Christ."

Who is going to stand before the judgment seat of Christ? A brother. A Christian. Not unbelievers.

In 2 Corinthians 5:10 we read, "For we must all appear before the judgment seat of Christ, that each one may receive the things done in the body, according to what he has done, whether good or bad."

Let's set the stage here so there's no confusion. The Bible describes two major judgments in the future. The first one to come, the Judgment Seat of Christ, will happen in heaven right after the Rapture, during the Tribulation on earth. Then, after the thousand-year reign of Christ upon the earth, comes the Great White Throne Judgment, when unbelievers will be judged for their sin. Don't confuse the two. No unbeliever will stand before the Judgment Seat of Christ. They will be reserved for the Great White Throne Judgment later on in the future.

This Is Not About God's Judgment of the Believer's Sin

The Judgment Seat of Christ is not about the judgment for your sin. The Bible tells us that judgment already took place at the cross of Jesus Christ. There is nothing anyone can ever do to you about your sin because God did it to His Son on your behalf. Christ was condemned for us. That is what we read in Galatians 1:4: "Who gave himself for our sins, that He might deliver us from this present evil age." The Judgment Seat is not for judgment of your sin if you are a Christian.

This Is Not About a Believer's Judgment of Any Other Believer

Christians are good at judging other people. But we ought to remind ourselves that God has not called any of us to judge anyone else. Because all believers must stand before the Judgment Seat of Christ, each giving account of himself to God, we have no right to judge the work of other believers.

First Corinthians 4:5 warns, "Therefore judge nothing before the time, until the Lord comes, who will both bring to light the hidden things of darkness and reveal the counsels of the hearts. Then each one's praise will come from God." Christ will do that, and we'll receive rewards based on how we lived our lives as Christians. Let's look at these rewards.

THE REWARDS FOR BELIEVERS' WORKS

The Crown of the Victor

First of all, there is what we might call the victor's crown (1 Corinthians 9:25–27): "And everyone who competes for the prize is temperate in all things. Now they do it to obtain a perishable crown, but we for an imperishable crown. Therefore I run thus: not with uncertainty. Thus I fight: not as one who beats the air. But I discipline my body and bring it into subjection, lest when I have preached to others, I myself should become disqualified."

Paul speaks here about an imperishable crown. He says, "This is the crown I am going after." He uses an image that was very clear to the Corinthian believers reading his letter. The Corinthians had two great athletic events in their time. One was the Olympic Games, and the other was the Isthmian Games. The Isthmian Games were held at Corinth, so Paul's readers would be very familiar with them.

Contestants in the games had to go through rigorous training for ten months. The last month was spent in Corinth and was supervised daily by the judges in the gymnasium and on the athletic fields. The race was always a major attraction at the games, and that is the figure Paul uses to illustrate the faithful Christian life. He says that in a race, everyone runs, but only one receives the prize. The prize indicates that the apostle had in mind service and awards.

The Isthmian athletes worked so diligently for so long to gain only an insignificant prize (a perishable crown of leaves) that Paul's thought is, "How much more should we as Christians take control of our bodies, our energies, our motives, and our purposes, and discipline ourselves to be useful servants of God?"

Paul and Peter would agree that we Christians ought to discipline ourselves because, according to 1 Peter 1:4–5, we have "an inheritance incorruptible and undefiled and that does not fade away, reserved in heaven for you, who are kept by the power of God through faith for salvation ready to be revealed in the last time."

In addition to the victor's crown is the crown of rejoicing.

The Crown of Rejoicing

This is what we call the soul-winner's crown. In 1 Thessalonians 2:19 we read: "For what is our hope, or joy, or crown of rejoicing? Is it not even you in the presence of our Lord Jesus Christ at His coming?" Christians who win people to Christ will be rewarded. And when they get to heaven, the Bible says that the people they have won to Christ will be their crowns.

The Crown of Righteousness

Those who endure testing will receive a crown of righteousness. Some of us have been through some pretty tough things in our lives, and the crown of righteousness is for those who love His appearing. Second Timothy 4:8 says, "Finally, there is laid up for me the crown of righteousness, which the Lord, the righteous Judge, will give to me on that Day, and not to me only but also to all who have loved His appearing."

Those who look forward to Jesus' coming back will get this crown. It may not take long to hand those out because so many are caught up in staying here now. But a lot of Christians do look forward to the Lord's return, and they will be given a crown for it.

The Crown of Life

Revelation 2:10 says , "Do not fear any of those things which you are about to suffer. Indeed, the devil is about to throw some of you into prison, that you may be tested, and you will have tribulation ten days. Be faithful until death, and I will give you the crown of life."

Christians who are being martyred in China, Indonesia, and all over the world are going to stand before the Lord at the Judgment Seat of Christ and be handed the martyr's crown because they paid for their faith with their very lives.

The Crown of Glory

This crown apparently is for pastors and leaders. In 1 Peter 5:4 we read, "And when the Chief Shepherd appears, you will receive the crown of glory that does not fade away." Those of us who teach the Word of God and shepherd God's people will get a crown of glory if we are faithful.

FOUR APPLICATIONS

Reject the Misconceptions

Whenever you hear teaching on this doctrine about rewards, my friends, always reject the two common misconceptions about it. Remember that:

1. Righteousness is not always rewarded materially, and
2. Suffering is not a certain sign of sin.

Remember That the Lord Himself Is Our Chief Reward

Don't ever forget this! When Abraham was coming back from his skirmish with Chedorlaomer, the king of Sodom wanted to give him some of the spoils from the first fight. But Abraham said, "I will take nothing, from a thread to a sandal strap" (Genesis 14:23). A few verses later, the Lord said to Abraham, "Do not be afraid, Abram. I am your shield, your exceedingly great reward" (15:1).

Aren't you glad the Lord is your reward?

Resist Doing Works Outwardly for a Reward

Remember Matthew 6:1, 3–4: "Take heed that you do not do your charitable deeds before men, to be seen by them. Otherwise you have no reward from your Father in heaven. . . . But when you do a charitable deed, do not let your left hand know what your right hand is doing, that your charitable deed may be in secret; and your Father who sees in secret will Himself reward you openly."

So while we are to be concerned about rewards and working for rewards, we shouldn't parade in front of people and say, "I did this!" The Bible says if we do that, we get our reward here and miss the one in heaven. The reward there is going to be better than any we could ever get here. Hold out for the good one!

Reflect on the Ultimate Goal of Rewards

And what are we going to do with these crowns when we get them? Let me remind you of Revelation 4:10–11: "The twenty-four elders fall down before Him who sits on the throne and worship Him who lives forever and ever, and cast their crowns before the throne, saying: 'You are worthy, O Lord, to receive glory and honor and power; for You created all things, and by Your will they exist and were created.'"

That will be one of the most awesome days that we ever have in our lives! Wouldn't it be terrible to see people walking up and putting their crowns at the feet of Jesus, and then to remember, "I had a chance to live my life that way, but I took the other way"? Wouldn't it be awful to go up empty-handed?

When I think about this, my heart says, "Lord God, help me to live my life for You in such a way that when I stand before You that day, I won't come with my hands empty; but I will have some crowns to lay at Your feet as a way of worshipping and adoring and honoring You at that great celebration in heaven."

Do business till Christ returns.

1. Read Matthew 19:16–30, noting especially verses 29–30.

   a. What did the man in verse 16 seek from Jesus?

   b. To what requirement did the man not object? (verses 17–20)

   c. Over what requirement did he stumble—and why?
      (verses 21–22)

   d. What is the focus of Jesus' comments to His disciples—
      and how did they react? (verses 23–25)

2. Read 1 Corinthians 3:11–15.

   a. What is the foundation Paul describes for building a true spiritual life? (verse 11)

   b. What will happen to the Christian whose works are consumed at the Judgment Seat of Christ? What will he lose? (verse 15)

   c. Do you anticipate losing, or gaining, rewards when your life is judged?

DID YOU KNOW?

C hristians will one day stand before the Judgment Seat of Christ (Greek *bema*, 2 Corinthians 5:10). *Bema* is rooted in *baino*, to walk, and originally meant a "step"—the ground covered by a foot when walking. Then it became a stone step, then a place to which one stepped up—a place of authority or judgment. It is this raised place, or platform, which became common in the New Testament world. It is mentioned a number of times with reference to Jewish and Roman rulers: Matthew 27:19; Acts 12:21; 18:12, 16–17; 25:6, 10, 17. Paul then applied this common term to the place where Christ will stand to judge the works of His followers in this life: Romans 14:10; 2 Corinthians 5:10.

Until I Come

Jesus' own words of warning and comfort bring depth and insight to the circumstances surrounding the End Times. With honest and straightforward language, Dr. Jeremiah helps you get a clear look at the signs of the times.

What in the World Is Going On?

The Rapture and the events surrounding it are just one of the key points in this important work by Dr. Jeremiah about the End Times. In this study he shines the light of God's Word on the prophetic path now unfolding before the church and the world.

Each series is also available with correlating CD audio albums.

For pricing information and ordering, contact us at www.DavidJeremiah.org or call (800) 947-1993.

STAY CONNECTED
TO DR. DAVID JEREMIAH

Take advantage of two great ways to let Dr. David Jeremiah give you spiritual direction every day! Both are absolutely FREE.

Turning Points Magazine and Devotional

Receive Dr. David Jeremiah's monthly magazine, *Turning Points* each month:

- Monthly study focus
- 48 pages of life-changing reading
- Relevant articles
- Special features
- Humor section
- Family section
- Daily devotional readings for each day of the month
- Bible study resource offers
- Live event schedule
- Radio & television information

Your Daily Turning Point E-Devotional

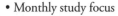

Start your day off right! Find words of inspiration and spiritual motivation waiting for you on your computer every morning! You can receive a daily e-devotional communication from David Jeremiah that will strengthen your walk with God and encourage you to live the authentic Christian life.

There are two easy ways to sign up for these free resources from Turning Point. Visit us online at www.DavidJeremiah.org and select "Subscribe to *Turning Points* Magazine" or visit the home page and find Daily Devotional to subscribe to your daily e-devotional.